WORKING IN SPORT

This book is a practical guide to getting your dream job in the sport industry. Offering a concise introduction to the contemporary sport industry and the wide range of careers within it, the book explains how to acquire the skills, qualifications, and experience you need to stand out from your competitors and start building your career in sport.

Covering all sectors of sport, from public to professional, from elite level to grassroots, and from major sports organizations to self-employment and entrepreneurship, the book surveys the landscape of the global sport industry. It looks at some of the myths that persist about working in sport and explains the types of education, qualifications, professional training, experiences, and skills that employers are looking for. The book identifies careers in different sectors of sport, such as sport management and sport media, and introduces the key building blocks of career development, including how to write a strong CV; good interview techniques; making the most of internships, placements, and volunteering; networking; and promoting your personal brand on social media. Every chapter includes interviews with successful industry professionals from around the world, and a "career playbook" section brings it all together with strategies and plans for taking those first steps forward.

This is essential reading for any student taking a sport-related course who wants to work in the sport industry as well as early career professionals looking to enhance their career prospects.

Rocco P. Porreca is Senior Lecturer at Oxford Brookes Business School, Oxford Brookes University, UK, and a former sport industry professional.

"*Working in Sport: A Practical Approach to Understanding Your Sport Journey* provides excellent insight into the sector of sport. Including over 20 interviews with sport industry professionals, the book provides a diverse range of commentary and career journey perspectives."

Dr. Stacie Gray, *Senior Lecturer in Sport Business and Leadership, University of Northampton, UK*

"This book provides essential insights into establishing a career in sports, incorporating perspectives from various industry stakeholders. It offers valuable advice for navigating the complexities of the sports sector and is essential reading for those seeking a career in the field."

Dr. Tom Bason, *Assistant Professor in Sport Management, Coventry University, UK*

"*Working in Sport* creates the foundation for anyone's journey into the sport industry. The author does a great job of incorporating his own viewpoints with those within the industry. A must read!"

Alexander Khilnani, *Senior Director of Yield Strategy, Revenue Innovation and Analytics, NBC Sports and Olympics*

WORKING IN SPORT

A Practical Approach to Understanding Your Sport Journey

Rocco P. Porreca

LONDON AND NEW YORK

Designed cover image: Getty Images / Far700

First published 2025

by Routledge
4 Park Square, Milton Park, Abingdon, Oxon OX14 4RN

and by Routledge
605 Third Avenue, New York, NY 10158

Routledge is an imprint of the Taylor & Francis Group, an informa business

© 2025 Rocco P. Porreca

The right of Rocco P. Porreca to be identified as author of this work has been asserted in accordance with sections 77 and 78 of the Copyright, Designs and Patents Act 1988.

All rights reserved. No part of this book may be reprinted or reproduced or utilised in any form or by any electronic, mechanical, or other means, now known or hereafter invented, including photocopying and recording, or in any information storage or retrieval system, without permission in writing from the publishers.

Trademark notice: Product or corporate names may be trademarks or registered trademarks, and are used only for identification and explanation without intent to infringe.

British Library Cataloguing-in-Publication Data
A catalogue record for this book is available from the British Library

ISBN: 978-1-032-48490-7 (hbk)
ISBN: 978-1-032-48489-1 (pbk)
ISBN: 978-1-003-38933-0 (ebk)

DOI: 10.4324/9781003389330

Typeset in Sabon
by Deanta Global Publishing Services, Chennai, India

Access the Support Material: www.routledge.com/9781032484891

For Enzo

CONTENTS

List of Action Items   *x*
Foreword   *xii*
Preface   *xiii*
Acknowledgments   *xv*
Chapter Image Credits   *xvi*

1   The Business of Sport: A Brief Introduction   1

2   Working in the Sport Industry: The Skills Needed   26

3   Why Do You Want to Work in the Sport Industry?   43

4   Understanding Your Path   56

5   Growth Mindset and Moving Forward: Accepting "No"   70

6   Gaining Experience: Importance and Where to Start   88

7   Your "Career Playbook": Putting It All Together   102

Appendices   *127*
Index   *129*

LIST OF ACTION ITEMS

Chapter 1

1 What Aspect of the Sport Industry Do You Want to Work in?

Chapter 2

2 What Skills Do You Need to Develop?

Chapter 3

3 My Strengths
4 My Values and Passions
5 Short- and Long-Term Goals
6 Why a Career in This Industry?

Chapter 4

7 Mapping Your Path to Working in Sport

Chapter 5

8   Growth Mindset
9   Anticipating Challenges
10 Preparing Your STAR Answer

Chapter 6

11 Your Plan for Gaining Experience

Chapter 7

12 Building a Network
13 Applicant Tracking System Keywords
14 Two Important Questions (and Answers)
15 Quote(s) of Interest
16 Quote(s) of Interest

FOREWORD

Embarking on a career journey is a monumental step, one that demands strategic planning, insightful decision-making, and a firm grasp of the landscape ahead. Whether you're a recent graduate venturing into the workforce for the first time or a seasoned professional seeking new horizons, understanding the nuances of the job search process is paramount. In "Working in Sport: A Practical Approach to Understanding Your Sport Journey" authored by Dr Rocco P. Porreca, readers are presented with a roadmap to navigate the intricate terrain of career exploration and development. Drawing from years of expertise and industry leadership, Dr Porreca illuminates the essential skills, strategies, and mindset necessary to thrive in the competitive realm of the sports industry.

Aspiring sports industry professionals are faced with a unique set of challenges when searching for a career in sports. Dr Porreca's book serves as a playbook, guiding readers through the unique characteristics of the sports industry. From dissecting the intricacies of sports business to unraveling the secrets of career advancement, each chapter is meticulously crafted to provide actionable insights and practical advice. Through a lens sharpened by real-world experience, Dr Porreca highlights the distinctive characteristics of the sports industry and offers invaluable wisdom on how to leverage these traits to carve out a successful career path. Whether you're drawn to the adrenaline of game day or the strategic maneuvers behind the scenes, this book equips you with the tools to thrive in the dynamic world of sports.

Dr Charles Barr, Professor of Sports Management,
Lynn University, USA

PREFACE

To the reader:
Working in sport is a journey. Trust the process and enjoy each step along the way.

Let me welcome you to the start of your sport journey. As you embark on this path, it is important to understand that the sport industry is competitive and is continuously growing. There are hundreds of sport-specific business and management programs that exist at universities across the globe. This results in thousands of students who graduate each year with the same goal: to work in sport. Unfortunately, the number of sport industry positions open each year does not correspond to the number of students entering the market. The supply simply does not meet the demand. Therefore, it is even more imperative for you to be prepared and to put yourself in the best possible position to compete for a job and career.

This book came about after reflecting on my own journey towards working in sport. Like many, my path to working in the industry was not linear. It was a journey filled with trial and error and ups and downs. But, mainly, it was a journey in which I felt I needed guidance. I needed direction and insight into how to best go about getting my foot in the door and starting a career in sport. Over the years, I have searched for mentors and asked as many questions as I could. After finally getting a break and getting my first opportunity as a full-time sport industry professional, I knew that someday I would aspire to help the next generation of those looking to work in sport. The way in which I would aim to help came into fruition as I transitioned from the sport industry to academia. I began teaching students who all had the same goals and dreams as me: to work in sport. It became evident that the best way to reach as many sport industry professional hopefuls as possible would be through writing a type of journey preparation guide filled with insight, guidance, and direction.

Working in Sport: A Practical Approach to Understanding Your Sport Journey is not designed to replace university instruction, nor should this be viewed as a traditional textbook. Instead, this book is designed to serve as an informative resource to combine one's knowledge of sport business concepts, theories, and the overall industry, with a dedicated guide for taking the next step towards your career. Further, this book is not written simply from my experience or opinion. This book is research-informed through over 20 interviews conducted with a diverse group of global sport business professionals covering 4 continents and 18 countries. The result, over 250 pages of transcribed data from more than 20 hours of interview time, all of which attributed to the content and direction of this book.

As you read through *Working in Sport: A Practical Approach to Understanding Your Sport Journey*, you will find each chapter presenting specific "action items" for you to complete. These activities will help you to begin outlining your path to working in the sport industry, while also helping to create a specific strategy for moving forward in the process. The aim of this book is to provide you, the aspiring sport industry professional, with a practical guide and defined strategy for taking your first steps towards achieving your goals.

ACKNOWLEDGMENTS

To my family, thank you for setting me on a path to explore the world in my own way. You prepared me to take on the challenge, to make independent decisions, and to follow my dreams of working in sport. Without your continued support I would not have been able to embark on my own journey of ups and downs, while constantly pursuing a life of attempting to overachieve.

To my wife, thank you for believing in me more than I believe in myself. You are constantly telling me and others how great I am. While I am aware I am unremarkable in many ways, you have never let me feel that way. Thank you for pushing me to be more self-confident and the best version of myself on a daily basis. You have remained immensely patient over the last couple of years in which we have talked about this book, on almost a daily basis. Despite my own recognition of how unappealing those constant conversations may be in your eyes, you have always approached each conversation as if I was telling you about the book for the first time.

Finally, to all of my former students who asked for meetings outside of class to simply share your dreams and desires of working in the sport industry while also asking many of the same questions I have asked professors and mentors of mine over the years. These conversations lit the proverbial light bulb above my head showcasing the need for this type of information to be readily available on a wider scale. Keep asking questions and keep moving forward.

CHAPTER IMAGE CREDITS

Chapter 1   Shutterstock/NikomMaelao Production
Chapter 2   Shutterstock/Claudio Dickson
Chapter 3   Shutterstock/Sergey Pekar
Chapter 4   Shutterstock/ViValenty
Chapter 5   Shutterstock/Askhat Gilyakhov
Chapter 6   Shutterstock/Glebova Natalia
Chapter 7   Shutterstock/Valenty

1
THE BUSINESS OF SPORT
A Brief Introduction

Introduction

The book *Modern Sports Administration* by Dr James Mason, written in 1988, was dedicated to Walter O'Malley, the former owner of the Brooklyn Dodgers of Major League Baseball. Walter O'Malley is most famously known as a baseball pioneer. O'Malley helped revolutionize the game of baseball by relocating the Dodgers to Los Angeles in 1958, thus expanding Major League Baseball to the west coast of the United States. Despite O'Malley's influence on the game of baseball, he also played a major part in sport management becoming an academic discipline. In his book, Dr James Mason wrote:

DOI: 10.4324/9781003389330-1

This book is dedicated to Walter O'Malley, deceased former owner of the Los Angeles Dodgers Professional Baseball Team, whose creativity, vision, and foresight advanced the idea that sports administrators need academic preparation.

(WalterOmalley.com, 2023)

O'Malley could sense the impending growth of professional sport and ultimately its need for well-trained sport administration professionals (Pedersen & Thibault, 2019, p. 6). In a letter to Mason, O'Malley wrote:

Where would one go to find a person who, by virtue of education, has been trained to administer a stadium...or a person to fill an executive position at a team or league level?

(Brown & Kreutzer, 2001)

Mason would eventually respond to O'Malley's insightful letter and bring forth to life the first-ever Sport Administration program to Ohio University in 1966 (Masteralexis et al., 2015, p. 23). Since 1966, the number of sport management and business-related courses has grown exponentially. Currently, there are over 600 sport-related degree programs and courses offered at universities globally (DegreesInSports, 2023).

The industry of sport is one of the fastest-growing global industries. Burnand (2023) states that the sport economy in the United States is larger and produces more economic output than all but the 70 largest economies in the world combined. This growth, in terms of size and scope, has elevated the industry from recreation to commercialization and from commercialization to entertainment. As sport intertwines with the entertainment industry and ultimately keeps growing, a continuous desire to work in the industry exists. More and more students each year embark on an educational journey which aims to prepare them for a career in the sport industry. Even Harvard University (yes, that Harvard University) teaches a course entitled "The Business of Entertainment, Media, and Sports." A class that is highly desired and sought after, which focuses on decision-making and strategy execution in the sport and entertainment world (Harvard Business School, 2024).

O'Malley's forward-thinking and push for adequately trained sport business professionals in the 1960s is even more relevant today. As sport has turned into a multibillion-dollar industry, there is an increased need for competent business practice and ultimately for individuals educated and trained to work in this specialized industry (Gillentine & Crow, 2015, p. 1).

Career Opportunities or Directions

As you will read in Chapter 4, your start to working in the sport industry begins with a single step on a, somewhat, pre-identified path. However, prior to embarking on this journey and taking that first step, you need to know your options. The sport industry itself is vast, with a variety of avenues one can take to begin a career. The industry is made up of professional and recreational sport, amateur and grassroots sport, competition, apparel, and merchandise. Sport is a business that offers goods and services, and all activities and/or organizations which contribute to the facilitation, production, or promotion of sport can be considered as options for which one can work in.

As a reader, it is important to think about where in the sport industry you would like to work, or what about sport is of interest to you. Therefore, let's break down the sport industry into sections to best help you conceptualize your desired place in the industry. The following sections will start with a look into the private and public sectors, followed by an identification of potential career avenues within sport: Coaching, management, sales, entrepreneurship, and development. This is not an exhaustive list of career opportunities within the sport industry, but instead, a focused look at a few of the career categories in which those who were interviewed for this book hold or held positions within.

Sport: An Industry

As you have or, perhaps, will aim to study the business of sport, it is important to express the fact that despite sport being viewed and categorized as a business, sport should be labeled as an industry. A business, in itself, implies a focus on profit and the generation of revenue. While this is the case for many businesses operating in sport, there are businesses that focus on development or community, without the main focal point being revenue. These non-profit organizations are very much a part of the wider sport industry and act as viable avenues for careers in sport. As an industry, sport organizations within it serve a variety of functions. From the selling of the goods and services of globally recognized brands to the use of sport as a driver for peace and unity, sport is a complex industry. The complexities increase more so when there is an overlap between them. Take, for example, the International Olympic Committee (IOC). The IOC operates as a non-profit entity to use sport as a platform for peace and unity, but it also places an emphasis, unofficially, on generating revenue and growing a bottom line – as a business. Sport, as an industry, operates in a fast-moving environment which is subject to constant change.

The Three Sectors of Sport

Sport as an industry is comprised of a large number of business and organizations. Many of these business and organizations, despite operating in different aspects of the sport industry, are linked and work together. Therefore, to better understand the inner workings of the sport industry it can be discussed from the perspective of three distinct sectors: The private sector, the public sector, and the non-profit sector. By familiarizing yourself with the intricacies of the industry, you can best prepare yourself for starting a career in sport.

Private Sector

Real Madrid, the New York Yankees, and Nike are three of the most recognizable and valuable brands on the planet. These brands, among many others, are a part of the industry most are familiar with. They are a part of the private sector of the sport industry. This sector is easily recognizable for a specific reason; its commercial nature. However, it is important to point out that not all organizations operating in the private sector will mirror Nike or Real Madrid.

There is another segment to this sector, outside of professional sport, which is around privatized leisure and recreation. Many golf courses, tennis clubs, and fitness centers operate within this realm as well. With high fees and costs, leisure and recreation centers aim to provide excellent facilities along with an element of exclusivity for their members. Organizations within the private sector are focused on generating revenue and profits, and therefore the jobs within this industry are in place to help these organizations achieve success at the commercial level.

Entry-level positions around marketing, sales, and business development, for example, will be common within the private sector, as these positions directly align with the organization achieving strategic goals and objectives around revenue generation and profit.

Public Sector

The public sector of the sport industry encompasses national, state, regional, and local government agencies. These agencies assist in developing policy for sport and provide funding opportunities. Here sport is viewed as a service which is largely beneficial to society. Thus, governments and specialist agencies are willing to fund and invest in sport as a means of bettering communities and society at large. The public sector aims to provide affordable access to sport and leisure for as many as possible. Generated revenues are used to keep facilities, for example, up and running, while providing programming opportunities available for community members to participate in sport. Within the UK, the local councils aid in working with communities to promote sport and leisure opportunities through leisure centers, local schools, and other outlets. Similarly, to the private sector, many fitness centers, golf courses, and tennis clubs operate in this realm. These organizations differ in the public sector with its price offerings being viewed as much more affordable and less exclusive.

As example of a public sector organization in the UK is Sport England. This organization operates with a focus on creating a healthier England through the offering of sport. Career positions within this sector of the industry can fall around business development and strategy, for example.

Non-Profit Sector

Revenue generation is of high importance for the private sector; however, within the non-profit, or voluntary sector, the larger focus is on social objectives. The non-profit sector of the sport industry is traditionally made up of community-based organizations, governing bodies, and international sport organizations; these of which provide competition and participation opportunities, while also setting the rules of sport (e.g. International Olympic Committee). The non-profit sector can consist of individuals forming their own local sport club in their community or can consist of an organization like the IOC. One in which the staff who work there are paid a salary, and the revenues generated are stated to be used to fund their identified social objectives.

The non-profit sector includes a variety of sport career paths. These can include those found in the commercial sector, around sales, marketing, and communications, while also including positions with larger societal focuses, such as grassroot sport participation.

The Convergence of the Three Sectors

The three sectors are categorized independently of each other, but, in reality, overlap and operate at times together. For example, within the public sector, governments provide funding to non-profit organizations for sport development. In the UK, the government funds Sport England in the public sector to increase sport participation while also funding its non-profit sector counterpart, UK Sport, to develop elite sport. Both organizations also work together on initiatives which are mutually beneficial and aim to better sport in general such as safeguarding and well-being (UK Sport, 2023). Public sector agencies can also become involved in commercial sport through the support of stadium projects and regulatory frameworks for sport specific organizations, while both the public sector and non-profit sector support the private sector by developing and providing talent (e.g. athletes, coaches, and officials) (Hoye et al., 2009). Each of the three sectors are uniquely positioned to act independently of each other while also collaborating together.

Types of Jobs within the Sport Industry

Ruth, Gehrig, DiMaggio, Mantle…Costanza? Some of you may remember this statement from the television sitcom Seinfeld, when fictional character

George Costanza announced his new job as the Assistant to the Traveling Secretary for the New York Yankees to a stunned Jerry Seinfeld. The position seemed as far-fetched as the job offer itself. Despite the fictional nature of the job position for the New York Yankees, the fact that positions such as Traveling Secretary for a Major League Baseball club do exist, just ask Ben Tuliebitz of the New York Yankees (Hatch, 2016), the current version of a "traveling secretary."

Employment in the sport industry, despite its competitive nature, encompasses a variety of positions and career paths. There are numerous avenues to take as a volunteer, or during an internship or placement year, or as an entry-level candidate. Sport management and business-related university programs aim to prepare students to work in sport-related areas such as youth and recreational sport, high school or university sport, professional clubs, community centers, coaching, marketing, sales, tourism, and retail, amongst others. Due to the variety and coverage of this in other resources, this section of the book will not cover all the types of positions one could have with a career in the sport industry and instead will focus on a variety of position categories held by those interviewed for this book:

- Sales
- Marketing and Sponsorship
- Strategy and Development
- Communications
- Coaching
- Entrepreneurship
- Chief Executive Officer
- Non-profit: Sport Foundations
- Player Relations and Services
- Data Analytics

The below sections are introductions to the positions and not an in-depth analysis of each. As you will see during your studies or through your own research, there are numerous books and writings pertaining to each of the categories below specifically. Therefore, the intention here is to simply provide a glimpse into the world of sales or marketing, for example, and highlight the key function of each category, any trends to be on the lookout for, and the key skills needed to work in that area of sport. The level of experience needed for each position varies as well. From an internship or volunteer perspective, the amount of experience needed will be minimal. Moving towards an entry-level opportunity, there will be an expectation that the candidate has some experience (e.g. minimum of 1–2 years); however, this can also vary depending on the hiring organization and the duties and responsibilities associated with the role. In terms of education, entry-level positions will require a bachelor's degree, with many preferring a master's degree.

Sales

As a student, it was advised that working in sales was the way to break into the sport industry. The advice came from a professor of mine who, when "selling" us about sales, often wore his two Super Bowl rings from the 1998 and 1999 Denver Broncos; both of which were acquired as a member of the ticket sales department and not as a player. From that point on, sales as a way into the sport industry, seemed legitimate and interesting. However, not all aspects of working in sales leads to the acquisition of a Super Bowl ring. Instead, sales provide a vital component to the life of the industry at all levels. Whether it is selling sponsorship space to a local business to help support a youth baseball team, or selling hospitality experiences for a Premier League football club, sales is a necessary lifeblood.

> …don't be afraid to get your hands dirty…at the end of the day, if it helps you sell a ticket, or if it helps you create a little bit of a relationship that drives more tickets, go out and do it.
> *Alex Strafer, Account Executive Group Sales, DC United*

Primary Function

Sport itself is a product, and as a product it needs to be purchased and consumed in some way, shape, or form. Those working in sales in the sport industry are tasked with the role of encouraging consumers to purchase the product or products they are selling. Whether that product is a ticket to a sporting event, merchandise to a fan, or a tennis racket to a recreational player, sales is a vital component to the continued growth of the industry. For organizations whose primary sales function is that of selling tickets, sales can also impact other departments within the organization. Selling tickets, in this case, not only generates revenue for the organization, but the team in charge of selling is also tasked with developing relationships with customers, and aiding in messaging used by the marketing team (Popp et al., 2017).

Trends to Keep in Mind

Sales, like other functions within the sport industry, is subject to a changing environment; this is especially evident in sales. The ways in which consumers purchase tickets and the way in which organizations present tickets as tangible products have changed. There is an increase, for example, in sport clubs only accepting digital tickets for fans attending matches. Long gone are the days of physical paper tickets. As a result, digital tickets have improved the consumer experience while also taking away the souvenir and memory associated with physical tickets. The Chicago Blackhawks of the NHL are one sport organization, who have recognized the desire of physical tickets among some of their fanbase and in conjunction with the ticketing and sales department created the Blackhawks Classics program (Joyce, 2024). Here fans can buy physical tickets with a QR code embedded to capture special moments from the game. Fans can scan the QR code and re-watch/experience the memorable moment from the game. Sales is about selling a product, but within sport, it can also very much be about selling an experience.

Key Skills Needed

Communication, Creativity, Interpersonal Skills, Willingness to Work Outside Normal Hours

Marketing and Sponsorship

Careers within the realm of marketing and sponsorship were the most prevalent amongst those interviewed for this book. Over 25% of the interviewees either work in or have worked in marketing and sponsorship throughout their careers in the sport industry. So, what does this tell you? Marketing and sponsorship both play a significant role in the industry, and there are a number of viable career paths associated with either.

Primary Function

The marketing of sport covers a lot. Athletes, teams and clubs, and products and services all need to be marketed. The process of marketing in sport is to create a level of interest and attraction amongst consumers. Chadwick and Beech (2007) define sport marketing as "an ongoing process through which contests with an uncertain outcome are staged creating opportunities for the simultaneous fulfilment of direct and indirect objectives amongst sport consumers, sport businesses and other related individuals and organizations." When marketing is concerned with a sporting event, the element of uncertainty (e.g. Who will win? What will happen during the contest?) creates a unique platform from which marketers can sell and promote sport. However, sport marketing also needs to be associated with the marketing of sport outside of sporting events. Nike needs to market its latest running shoes, Wilson needs to market its newest tennis racket, and a recreation center needs to market its class offerings. Certainly, Nike and Wilson will align their latest product offerings with an athlete, but the point being, is that sport marketing is easily associated with competitive sport, but there are other options within marketing, outside of competitive sport, for you to have a career in. The impact that marketing can have on an organization is tremendous. Thus, expenditures from marketing efforts can be quite high in sport. For example, from 2014 to 2023 Nike spent just under $35 billion in worldwide marketing costs (Nike, 2023a), resulting in a generated revenue of roughly $380 billion during the same period (Nike, 2023b).

Sponsorship, a segment of marketing, is about promotion through connection. Brands align and connect themselves with a sport entity, and vice versa, to create a reciprocating relationship. Sahnoun (1989) simply refers to sponsorship as a tool. A tool which links brands (companies and organizations) to specific audiences and/or attractive events. Take Airbnb and the Olympics, for example. Two brands which are inherently different, yet uniquely linked together through sponsorship. Airbnb is a major sponsor of the Olympic Games and has been since 2019 (IOC, 2019). The sponsorship came together around a similar set of ideals on sustainability and hosting, yet there is a mutually beneficial aspect of the sponsorship as well: Revenue for the IOC and visibility for Airbnb through specific audiences (sport fans). To further highlight the association around specific audiences and events, in Europe in 2022, 63% of all sport sponsorship deals were with teams, and 21% were with events (Strive, 2023).

Trends to Keep in Mind

> Goodform is a marketing agency that helps sport organizations based on data; to improve the value of that data…to create personalized content and be more engaging with the fans.
> *Alvaro Revilla, Client Manager, Goodform*

With the influx and evolution of technology, marketing and sponsorship have become more data driven. Data analytics are being used more to inform an organization's decision-making, to measure marketing initiatives and sponsorship impact, and to further engage with consumers and fans. A key function of marketing is to understand your audience. Through data analysis, organizations can better understand the preferences, behaviors, and needs of their consumer-base, thus, allowing for organizations to create more relevant marketing materials and appealing sponsorships. Those looking to get involved in marketing and sponsorship should be aware of the use of and need for data-driven insight and digitalized or hybrid-based experiences to complement a marketing or sponsorship initiative.

Key Skills Needed

Communication, Collaboration, Creativity, Data Analytics, Willingness to Work Outside Normal Hours

Strategy and Development

Primary Function

Go to the website of any sport organization and it is likely you will be able to find their current strategic plan. These strategic plans consist of a number of set initiatives the organization will aim to accomplish over a set period of time. Whether short or long-term goals, organizations within the sport industry will have a clear strategic plan in place on how the business itself can further develop and grow. The objectives of the organization will correspond with its overall mission and vision. However, strategies can differ depending on the type of organization and the sector in which it resides. Using the example of USA Football, a national sport governing body, it has set strategic goals in place around four key areas of highlighted importance: Development, safety, values, and participation (USA Football, 2023). In this case there are elements of organizational strategy (e.g. values and safety) mixed with the development (e.g. participation) of sport at a variety of levels (recreational, amateur, Olympic) for a number of different athletes.

> I oversee our development arms, so we have an approximately $2,000,000 grant fund that we use to support individual athletes, leagues and organizations that are furthering football within the United States and who come from areas that are not economically strong. So, people that are just disadvantaged and or otherwise would have limited participation due to finances. And so, we supply support in the form of financial grants, we do equipment grants where we provide equipment, basic equipment.... And then I also oversee our philanthropic arms, so any of our philanthropic activities, as well as any additional strategic objectives.
>
> Beth Porreca, Managing Director High Performance and National Teams, USA Football

Think of strategy and development as a wheel in the operations of an organization. That wheel has a number of cogs serving as job roles which aid in making the operational wheel turn. From a career perspective there are numerous positions which fall under the umbrella of strategy and development. These positions can be very niche and focused, such as organizing player development camps in the northeastern part of the country for USA Football to grow its youth participation levels. Alternatively, positions at a broader organizational level, such as new business development, focus on searching for sponsorship opportunities to bring in additional revenue. Despite the role you will have working in sport, it will contribute, in some way, to the strategic goals and objectives of the organization.

Trends to Keep in Mind

Strategic and developmental initiatives are also subject to the evolution of the sport industry. Organizations need to be aware of movements in the industry and align objectives with current trends. Deloitte's (2023) Future of Sport report highlights six key forces which are shaping the future of sport:

1. Evolution of the global sports market
2. Next generation of fans
3. Influence of digitalization
4. Diversity, equity, and inclusion
5. Health and well-being
6. Environmental sustainability

Most larger organizations within the industry are going to focus on all six of these key forces, whereas smaller organizations may only be concerned with a few. Either way, if you want to have a career in the sport industry you need to stay up-to-date with current trends and how those trends are or can impact the aspect of sport industry in which you are working. Even if you do not want to have a career which specifically focuses on strategy or development, the organization you will work for will certainly have a strategic focus.

Key Skills Needed

Organization, Communication, Teamwork, Passion, Willingness to Work Outside Normal Hours

Communications

Primary Function

Sport is a consumer-focused industry. As such, a primary responsibility of sport organizations is to communicate with its consumers and stakeholders. The role of communications within the sport industry can therefore encompass a number of areas. For example, public relations, research, broadcasting, social and digital media, podcasting, community relations, partnerships, and memberships, among others.

> My official role is sport communications and media relations manager. So, in my role I oversee all media operations on major events. Especially, the World Championships, World Cup Finals, European Championships and Olympic Games. And also, to liaise with all the journalists that cover equestrian from a sports side. So that means that I don't cover any

corporate political side of the federation. This is some other colleagues within the communications team, but I just focus solely on the sports side of communications.

Didier Montes Kienle, Manager, Sport Communications and Media Relations, Fédération Équestre Internationale (FEI)

The communications department can have a direct impact on the image of the organization, its ability to engage with and inform consumers, and on revenue generation. The majority of sport organizations exist as visible brands. Through content creation, social and digital media management, and public relations, the communications department plays a large role in preserving and enhancing the image of the organization. These efforts can also directly impact the fans and stakeholders of the organization. Consumer engagement is critical to the sport industry and as such those in communications aid in developing and maintaining a bond between consumer and organization.

Not all communication efforts from a sport organization will focus on the positives of the business. At times, especially due to the high-profile nature of much of the sport industry, public controversy or crisis occur. The communications team will assist in the immediate response of an unforeseen event or controversy. This is to ensure the organization's image is best preserved and that consumers and fans are informed in a transparent manner.

Trends to Keep in Mind

Key trends within the communication department is keeping up with how consumers and fans absorb information, especially in the continuing age of digitalization. What communication outlets are most used amongst key target demographics? As highlighted earlier, the Gen Z and Gen Alpha demographic is entering and will become a dominant consumer base in the sport industry. The Gen Z market prefers to consume information via social media platforms, such as TikTok. Therefore, those in a communication role need to understand how to best reach their target demographic effectively. Further, communication from sport organization to consumer is moving from solely an informational basis to that of an informational and immersive experience. Consumers want to interact with the organization as opposed to simply being informed. In 2022 the International Equestrian Federation (FEI) formed its own TikTok channel: FEI Horse World. This channel came following the success of previous digital media channels on YouTube and Instagram, and through the understanding of how to reach a younger audience. In the first three months, the FEI TikTok channel gained

36,000 followers. From there the channel garnered 7.9 million views and over 900,000 engagements (FEI, 2022).

Key Skills Needed

Developed soft skills: How to interact with people – communication and interpersonal skills. Attention to Detail, Time Management, Social Media, Willingness to Work Outside Normal Hours

Coaching

Primary Function

Sport coaching, as a profession, has many avenues one can take to become involved in this aspect of the industry. Coaches can be self-employed, or employed through an organization. Coaches can work within professional sport, recreational sport, or grassroots sport. Within these three categories of sport, one can work for a professional team or player, a recreational athletic or leisure facility, or within the local community.

According to a 2024 *IBISWorld* report, 322,639 people were employed as sport coaches in the United States. The industry itself generated $15 billion with a growth rate of just under 4% from 2018 to 2023 and with a projected growth rate of almost 3% from 2023 to 2028. It is a section of the sport industry that is growing and filled with opportunities. However, it is worth identifying that not all coaching roles will pay the same. Coaching positions with grassroots sport or at a recreational level will typically be lower paying or volunteer positions. Higher levels of sport (e.g. elite, collegiate) come with more exclusivity and higher pay; however, these positions also demand the most experience and are the most competitive.

Trends to Keep in Mind

As with many of the career routes discussed, technology is playing a large part in the growth and evolution of the industry. Coaching is not exempt from this. The ways in which coaches can use technology, from breaking down a video of a swing or shot, to the dissection of data from a history of performances, to the potential for artificial intelligence to create virtual training environments, have enhanced the profession. Further, there is a strong emphasis on coaching licenses, certifications, and compliance.

> I have my United States Soccer Federation (USSF) coaching license…I am personal trainer certified and nutrition certified.
> *Elise Cloutier, Marketing, Youth Program &*
> *Business Development Director for Liverpool*
> *Football Club International Academies*

Further, the coaching profession does not need to focus solely on teaching specific technical skills for a particular sport. Coaching now encompasses all aspects of performance, including the mental side of playing.

> I thought I was going to be a coach...So I was coaching all along and I enjoyed it, but I didn't really have much understanding on how to be a good coach. (Then, I was) introduced to this idea of sports psychology.
> *Dr Larry Lauer, Director of Mental Performance, United States Tennis Association (USTA)*

Key Skills Needed

Sport Knowledge/Playing Experience, Communication*, Interpersonal Skills, Technology, Coaching License/Certification, Willingness to Work Outside Normal Hours

> *Because most of what we do is sort of separated, you prepare the athletes, watch them perform, only then to get feedback afterwards.
> *Dr Larry Lauer, Director of Mental Performance, United States Tennis Association (USTA)*

Entrepreneurship

Primary Function

Not everyone who aspires to have a career in sport wants to work for a sport organization. Instead, some want to be their own boss, start up their own company, and be an entrepreneur. As you will read in Chapter 4, it is imperative to go about your sport journey with an entrepreneurial mindset. Therefore, each of you reading this book and looking to start your career journey will already possess a bit of entrepreneurial spirit should you decide to go down the route of starting your own sport business.

It can be argued that entrepreneurship is universal in all industries; however, as we know, the sport industry is unique. Therefore, sport entrepreneurship should be identified independently of other forms of entrepreneurship. Bill (2009) defines a sport entrepreneur as an innovative and creative individual with a sport industry-specific level of knowledge who can spot and generate openings in the sport sector while recognizing and taking advantage of market opportunities. Further, it is important to include that entrepreneurs assume and take risks.

Entrepreneurs, especially in the sport industry, look for new ways to present a product, or search for new markets for a current or new product. Entrepreneurs use their skill set to navigate uncertainty and see problems or issues as opportunities. Entrepreneurs seek chance, take initiative, calculate risk, think creatively, and make decisions.

> It's funny because I'm still debating whether I'm entrepreneurial or I'm creative, because I would say more the latter. In a sense, that's what I think. What really drives (me) is creating things…there's a lot of entrepreneurial spirit there. There's a lot of creative spirit there as well.
>
> *Joao Frigerio, Founder, iWorkinSport*

Trends to Keep in Mind

Entrepreneurs search for opportunity and chance. A major part of recognizing an opportunity is to keep up with where the industry is going: What trends are prominent now and potentially into the future? Recently, there has been significant growth in technology in and around the sport industry such as non-fungible tokens (NFTs) (e.g. Liverpool Football Club), cryptoassets (e.g. Socios fan tokens), artificial intelligence, the metaverse (e.g. Brooklyn Nets – Netaverse), and blockchain (e.g. potential to revolutionize players transfers). These trends resulted in an influx of crypto-related business looking to involve themselves in the sport industry (Bason et al., 2023).

There is a new generation of fans entering and consuming sport: Generation Z (Gen Z) and Generation Alpha (Gen Alpha). Both sets of fans have been born into a technological age, with the Gen Alpha consumers, as the youngest, growing up in an age of TikTok influence, and the growth of AI and 5G (Deloitte, 2023). As a result, we have seen sport leagues change formats to be more quickly consumed (e.g. Cricket) as well as alter the way in which fans are introduced to sport (e.g. Netflix and Drive to Survive for Formula One). Entrepreneurs entering the sport industry need to also be aware of the future impact of digitalization on sport. Artificial intelligence, the metaverse, and Web 3.0 are in an infancy stage with future growth predicted, resulting in an altering of the way in which sport is consumed, and how sport organizations engage with fans.

Key Skills Needed

Problem Solving, Decision-Making, Creativity, Communication, Sales, Negotiation, Willingness to Work Outside Normal Hours

Chief Executive Officer

Primary Function

The role of a Chief Executive Officer, also known as a Chief Executive or CEO, is a role which comes with time and experience. As you embark on your career in the sport industry a role such as this is the aspiration or end goal of the journey; it is not the starting point. For some, you may be looking to transition careers and perhaps you have enough experience in another industry which qualifies you for a CEO role in sport now, but for those just starting out you will need to build your experiences over time to prepare for becoming a Chief Executive. To put this into perspective, the individual interviewed for this book, who is currently a Chief Executive in the sport industry, began this career journey over 30 years ago, amassing significant experience along the way.

A Chief Executive must deliver an organization's mission and vision through goal setting, foresight, and decision-making. It is expected that the individual in the role has a strong understanding of the current strategy of the organization, has the ability to lead, understands the law, rules, and regulations within the industry, and can mitigate risk and make decisions.

> You need to have a very high degree of self-motivation and resilience.
> *Anonymous, Chief Executive Officer*

Carolyn Radford, the current Chief Executive for Mansfield Town Football Club, a UK-based club currently playing in League Two of the English Football League, describes her day as one filled with meetings and interactions. On a daily basis, Radford meets with department heads, players, and coaching staff. She works through club finances and recruitment while also discussing safety and match control with the relevant parties. Finally, to close out the day, unless there is a match and she needs to speak with the grounds crew, Radford meets with the sponsors of the club (Meyerowitz, 2018). As Chief Executive, Radford has her hand in all aspects of the business, from the playing and performance side to the marketing and commercial side. Working in this role requires a very deep and well-rounded set of skills.

Trends to Keep in Mind

As a Chief Executive you need to be aware of trends and changes in the industry that impact the organization as a whole. With the other positions, the focus is more so on trends in the industry which then impact the way in which your immediate department operates (e.g. selling tickets or putting together a marketing campaign). Here, you need to be aware of trends impacting sport holistically and think back to how this can impact your organization. Refer back to Deloitte's (2023) Future of Sport and its six key forces:

1. Evolution of the global sports market
2. Next generation of fans
3. Influence of digitalization
4. Diversity, equity, and inclusion
5. Health and well-being
6. Environmental sustainability

How will these six areas impact the stakeholders of your organization? A football club, for example, is going to have a variety of stakeholders: Fans, sponsors, a board, players, governing body, league, employees, etc.. These stakeholders are going to be impacted by or are perhaps leading the change for the future of sport. For example, due to the influx of technology fans are going to be expecting more immersive experiences to consume sport; employees are going to need additional skills around data and analytics. The Chief Executive will need to recognize this and then put a plan in action to meet the needs of the future.

Key Skills Needed

Knowledge of Law, Decision-Making, Communication, Vision, Leadership, Willingness to Work Outside Normal Hours

Non-Profit: Sport Foundations

Primary Function

It is easy to get caught up in the exciting nature of commercial sport and the continued desire to generate fan engagement and higher amounts of revenue on a yearly basis. Yet, for many, sport is not just a business but a driver for change and doing good. Careers within the non-profit component of the sport industry have a greater focus on the work being done and the social objectives associated with it. Take for example the Fédération Internationale de Basketball or FIBA – the International Basketball Federation. FIBA is the governing body for the sport of basketball on a global level. Within FIBA is the FIBA Foundation, which is the "social legacy arm" of the international governing body. The FIBA Foundation focuses on the role that basketball plays in society, while promoting and preserving the values and history associated with the sport (FIBA, 2024). In 2016, the FIBA Foundation began its

Basketball for Good program, which aims to unite communities through multiple initiatives, such as its youth engagement programs that promote education, health, and equality. The Basketball for Good program has impacts over 95,000 people per year in 158 different countries (FIBA, 2024).

> And I felt that this was exactly what I was looking for, bridging the two passions I had of sports and social impact. (At the FIBA Foundation we) work with different people, not only within our office, but our regional offices and every continent and as well as our national federations and every country we have 212 member federations as well as other actors in this sport for development field, which many people do not know the difference between sport development, which is mainly just focused on the sport side and sport for development, which is using the sport as a tool to address social issues that are relevant in the country.
>
> *Theren Bullock, Foundation Senior Manager,*
> *Fédération Internationale de Basketball (FIBA)*

Trends to Keep in Mind

As the sport industry moves forward, there will be an increasing focus on diversity, equity, inclusion, health, well-being, and environmental sustainability (Deloitte, 2023). Therefore, the focus on using sport for development in those areas will persist. If you are looking to work in the non-profit sector, specifically with a sport foundation or governing body, you will need to familiarize yourself with the United Nations' (2024) Sustainable Development Goals (SDGs). The current SDGs are located below in Table 1.1. Non-profit organizations, such as the FIBA Foundation, are aligning objectives and future goals

TABLE 1.1 Sustainable Development Goals of the United Nations

SDG 1: No poverty	SDG 10: Reduced inequalities
SDG 2: Zero hunger	SDG 11: Sustainable cities and communities
SDG 3: Good health and well-being	
SDG 4: Quality education	SDG 12: Responsible consumption and production
SDG 5: Gender equality	
SDG 6: Clean water and sanitation	SDG 13: Climate action
SDG 7: Affordable and clean energy	SDG 14: Life below water
SDG 8: Decent work and economic growth	SDG 15: Life on land
	SDG 16: Peace, justice, and strong institutions
SDG 9: Industry, innovation and infrastructure	**SDG 17: Partnerships for the goals**

with specific SDGs (FIBA Foundation's in bold). Therefore, a general understanding of the goals and how they are currently aligning with or how they can influence a future direction of the organization can be beneficial when applying and interviewing for a position with a sport foundation or non-profit organization.

Key Skills Needed

Organization, Planning, Understanding of SDGs, Communication, Teamwork, Willingness to Work Outside Normal Hours

Player Relations and Services

Primary Function

Player relations and services can be simply categorized as a form of player operations. Those working in these types of roles will need to understand the strategic direction of the organization in relation to the player aspect, which is a part of it. Similar to many of the other roles identified, a player relations and services role can encompass a variety of categories. For example, coaching, physical therapy and athletic training, equipment, member services, analytics, scouting, anti-doping, and player development, among others. Therefore, in this career, you can be working directly with the players and athletes (e.g. mental skills, video analysis), or indirectly (e.g. travel coordination, talent identification camp planning).

> I was a coordinator of business services...We expanded to host our junior players, so it was also a full year-round facility so that players could stay at our dormitories. So, in doing that, there was a lot of other duties and responsibilities that came with this. With the training center, and so I stepped in to quite a few different places that were needed and assisted with certain aspects of the dorms. But then I did a little bit of everything in my role. I assisted with the human resources side of the staffing, assisted with training for new or the new expense report process or the website; I assisted in helping them to develop and grow the new website format...a majority of our events. I had a hand in our local tournaments and things that were on site. So, my hands were in a lot of different areas; facility management, anything that had to do with the travel for the collegiate team and assisting with the international collegiate annual event.
> *Kristiana Bennett, formerly of the United States Tennis Association (USTA)*

Due to the direct and indirect nature of the positions with regard to players and athletes, a variety of skills are needed. Many of these roles can be administrative based with a strong focus on customer service and event planning.

Trends to Keep in Mind

Diversity, equity, and inclusion (DEI) was an identified future trend to focus on in the sport industry (Deliotte, 2023). From a player relations and services standpoint, there will be a push in these areas. This includes a stronger promotion of DEI awareness and initiatives, more equitable gender participation in sport, enhanced equitable media coverage of men's and women's sport, and the continued growth of women's sport in general. Depending on the career path taken within player relations and services DEI efforts could look differently. For example, on an administrative side this could be around more diverse staffing across all areas, or from a player development standpoint, more focus on inclusive grassroots participation within talent identification.

Key Skills Needed

Customer Service, Communication, Adaptability, Interpersonal Skills, Willingness to Work Outside Normal Hours

Data Analytics

Primary Function

When we think of data analytics in the sport industry our first thought may go to the book, *Moneyball: The Art of Winning an Unfair Game* by Michael Lewis, or perhaps instead the movie *Moneyball*, both of which showcased the use of numbers (analytics) to predict performance and success in baseball. Data analytics has since encompassed all of sport. As Jarvis and Westcott (2020) state, "If measuring something in sports is conceivable, chances are that someone, somewhere is already measuring it." Data analytics in the sport industry has taken off over the last decade plus. From the performance side, most major professional sport clubs house an analytics person or department. However, data analytics is not limited to player or team performance.

Additionally, it can be used to transform the way in which organizations market themselves, sell products, communicate with stakeholders, and identify new business opportunities. Data analytics is being used by sport leagues to enhance fan engagement. For example, the Professional Squash Association (PSA) partnered with Red Zone to supply live data during professional squash tournament broadcasts during the 2023–2024 season (Saleh, 2023). This initiative aims to bring a holistic presentation of the sport to its viewers through in-depth shot and play analysis. Alternatively, the National Football League (NFL) has partnered with Genius Sports through the 2027–2028 season to exclusively distribute real-time data and statistics to sport betting companies as a means of enhancing fan engagement (NFL, 2023).

> …data analysis and data visualization and how you can maximize that in sports. It's focused probably on performance right, which is the training (aspect). But what we are doing here in Goodform is basically try to do those techniques for a more commercial and fan engagement side.
> *Alvaro Revilla, Client Manager, Goodform*

In addition to fan engagement, data analytics positions can focus on the overall business operations of the sport organization. From a position currently advertised by the United States Tennis Association as an entry-level data analyst, the candidate here will work closely with the business operations team and will be responsible for obtaining and analyzing data relating to facility operations, the Pro Shop, Campus Programs, and concessions (TeamWork Online, 2024).

Trends to Keep in Mind

As data collection and analysis continues to become more prevalent in the sport industry, an emphasis will be on privacy and data integrity. Data is being collected from a significant number of individuals associated with the sport industry, from a fan engagement side to a performance side (amateur and professional). It is predicted that by 2030, technology will be embedded across all areas of physical fitness and health (Deliotte, 2023). This includes providing athletes, coaches, and organizational staff with data collection tools to advise decision-making. Therefore, how that data is handled, who has access, and, ultimately, who owns the right to collected data will need to be clearly updated and articulated, especially as sport organizations continue to grow and expand the use of external partnerships to aid in that collection and analysis of data.

Key Skills Needed

Data Visualization Software (e.g. Tableau), Attention to Detail, Communication, Develop Data Models, Customer Service

Conclusion

There are a number of career avenues one can take when looking to work in the sport. Each of the career categories identified, sales, marketing and sponsorship, strategy and development, communications, coaching, entrepreneurship, chief executive, non-profits, player relations and services, and data analytics, comes with numerous paths one can go down to become involved in that aspect of the industry. At this stage in your journey, focus on identifying one or more of the sectors of sport you are interested in and the area or areas of sport you would like to work in. For example, do you want to work in an aspect of the sport industry which focuses on societal objectives? Or, perhaps, you want to work directly with athletes or engage directly with fans and consumers. Generating an understanding of where you may like to go, earlier on, will help you as you move along in the book and set the foundational stage for beginning your journey to working in the sport industry.

Action Item 1: What Aspect of the Sport Industry Do You Want to Work in?

One of the first steps towards a career in the sport industry is to simply identify what aspects of the industry are appealing to you. Therefore, for your first action item you are to identify five different areas of sport business in which you are interested. For example, marketing, sales, or player development. After you have identified the five aspects or career categories you are interested in, number them in order of importance, with 1 being the most important, and fill out the Table 1.2 below.

Were you able to find a specific job within the area of sport business that you are the most interested in? If not, do not be discouraged as perhaps you have identified a niche area of the industry. Later on, in this book you will read about gaining experience and working towards your career of interest.

Your final task for this chapter is to look up the identified contact person (e.g. person in your desired position currently) for your listed job and take a look at their experience. As you research the organization you aspire to work for, search on LinkedIn by using the organization's name and job title, or check out the organization's staff directory to locate the person currently in your desired position. This is your identified "contact person." How many years have they worked in this position? What other experiences or skills, unique to this person, present themselves to you? You will use this information to think about what amount of experience and what specific skills you may need to obtain this specific job in the future.

TABLE 1.2 Action Item 1

Ranking	Sport Business Area	Specific Job	Sport Organization	Contact Person; Experience Level	Skills
Example:	Player Development	Tennis Administrator	United States Tennis Association	John Smith; 3 years of experience	Highly organized; excellent communicator
1					
2					
3					
4					
5					

Further Resources

Deloitte. (2023). *The future of sport*. https://www2.deloitte.com/content/dam/Deloitte/uk/Documents/deloitte-uk-future-of-sport-report-updated.pdf
This report provides the reader with insider insight into how the sport industry is expected to change by 2030 and what the driving forces of change are.

Front Office Sports. https://frontofficesports.com/
A free, online resource covering the business of sport. The reader can use this resource to obtain daily and updated coverage of sport as a business.

LinkedIn. https://www.linkedin.com/
The first step to making contact in sport. A free form of professional social media allowing you to connect with peers in and around the industry.

References

Bason, T., Petratos, P., Porreca, R., & Mohiuddin Babu, M. (2023). Sport and blockchain. *The Centre for Business in Society White Paper Series*. Coventry University.

Beech, J., & Chadwick, S. (2007). Introduction: The marketing of sport. In *The marketing of sport* (pp. 4–5). Pearson. https://ci.nii.ac.jp/ncid/BA84698676

Bill, K. (2009). *Sport management*. Learning Matters.

Brown, M. T., & Kreutzer, A. (2001, December 24). Mason led the way in training sports execs. *Sports Business Journal*. https://www.sportsbusinessjournal.com/Journal/Issues/2001/12/24/Opinion/Mason-Led-The-Way-In-Training-Sports-Execs.aspx

Burnand, M. (2023, October). Why Saudi Arabia pours billions into sports (and it makes sense) [Audio podcast episode]. In *Economics Explained*. Spotify. https://open.spotify.com/episode/1MPxNNX2xX1OFAY0id4zPK

DegreesInSports. (2023). *Search sports degrees*. https://www.degreesinsports.com/search?k=&dt=&loc=1&campus=-1&p=1

Deloitte. (2023). *The future of sport*. https://www2.deloitte.com/content/dam/Deloitte/uk/Documents/deloitte-uk-future-of-sport-report-updated.pdf

FEI. (2022). *FEI Campaigns & Fan Engagement – FEI Annual Report 2022*. https://inside.fei.org/fei/about-fei/publications/fei-annual-report/2022/campaigns-fan-engagement/

FIBA. (2024). *FIBA Foundation*. https://www.fiba.basketball/foundation?page=/ibf/about

Gillentine, A., & Crow, R. B. (2015). *Foundations of sport management*. FiT Publishing.

Harvard Business School. (2024). *The Business of Entertainment, Media, and Sports – Executive Education - Harvard Business School*. HBS Executive Education. https://www.exed.hbs.edu/business-entertainment-media-sports/

Hatch, R. (2016, September 13). Behind the scenes with the Yankees' traveling secretary. *Thrillist*. https://www.thrillist.com/travel/nation/new-york-yankees-travel-ben-tuliebitz

Hoye, R., Smith, A., Nicholson, M., Stewart, B., & Westerbeek, H. (2009). Sport management. In *Sport management: Principles and applications* (p. 8). Routledge.

IBISWorld. (2024, March). *Sport coaching in the US*. https://my-ibisworld-com.oxfordbrookes.idm.oclc.org/us/en/industry/61162/industry-at-a-glance

IOC. (2019). *Airbnb – Official partner | Olympic Sponsors | IOC*. https://olympics.com/ioc/partners/airbnb

Jarvis, D., & Westcott, K. (2020, December 7). *The hyperquantified athlete: Technology, measurement, and the business of sports*. Deloitte Insights. https://www2.deloitte.com/uk/en/insights/industry/technology/technology-media-and-telecom-predictions/2021/athlete-data-analytics.html

Joyce, E. (2024, March 25). "Bring the Moment Home": Blackhawks fans can buy physical tickets embedded with highlights from game nights. *Sport Business Journal*. https://www.sportsbusinessjournal.com/Articles/2024/03/25/technology

Masteralexis, L. P., Barr, C. A., & Hums, M. A. (2015). *Principles and practice of sport management*. Jones & Bartlett Publishers.

Meyerowitz, A. (2018, January 9). A day in the life of: The CEO of professional football club. *Red Online*. https://www.redonline.co.uk/red-women/a530916/women-in-football-career-inspiration/

NFL. (2023, July 6). NFL extends strategic partnership with Genius Sports as exclusive official NFL data, Watch and Bet distribution partner. *NFL.com*. https://www.nfl.com/news/nfl-extends-strategic-partnership-with-genius-sports

Nike. (2023a, July 20). Nike's advertising and promotion costs from the financial years of 2014 to 2023 (in billion U.S. dollars) [Graph]. In *Statista*. Retrieved April 12, 2024, from https://www-statista-com.oxfordbrookes.idm.oclc.org/statistics/685734/nike-ad-spend/

Nike. (2023b, July 20). Nike's revenue worldwide from the fiscal years of 2005 to 2023 (in million U.S. dollars) [Graph]. In *Statista*. Retrieved April 12, 2024, from https://www-statista-com.oxfordbrookes.idm.oclc.org/statistics/241683/nikes-sales-worldwide-since-2004/

Pedersen, P. M., & Thibault, L. (2019). *Contemporary sport management* (6th ed.). Human Kinetics.

Popp, N., Simmons, J. M., & McEvoy, C. D. (2017). Sport ticket sales training: Perceived effectiveness and impact on ticket sales results. *Sport Marketing Quarterly*, 26(2), 99–109.

Sahnoun, P. (1989). *Le sponsoring: Mode d'emploi*. Chotard.

Saleh, T. (2023, August 24). PSA teams up with Red Zone to supply live data in broadcasts. *Sportcal*. https://www.sportcal.com/news/psa-teams-up-with-red-zone-to-supply-live-data-in-broadcasts/

Strive. (2023, April 21). Share of sports sponsorship deals in Europe in 2022, by type [Graph]. In *Statista*. Retrieved April 12, 2024, from https://www-statista-com.oxfordbrookes.idm.oclc.org/statistics/1448816/sports-sponsorship-europe-by-type/

TeamWork Online. (2024). *Data analyst and programs office associate – USTA*. https://www.teamworkonline.com/golf-tennis-jobs/protennisjobs/u-s--tennis--usta--29068/data-analyst-and-programs-office-associate-2077358

UK Sport. (2023, January 16). *UK sport and sport England move to strengthen safeguarding and welfare across sport*. https://www.uksport.gov.uk/news/2023/01/16/uk-sport-and-sport-england-move-to-strengthen-safeguarding-and-welfare-across-sport

United Nations. (2024). *THE 17 GOALS | Sustainable Development*. https://sdgs.un.org/goals

USA Football. (2023). *About USA football | Development | Values | Participation | Safety*. https://www.usafootball.com/about

WalterOMalley.com. (2023). *Walter O'Malley: Biography: Short stops: p*. https://www.walteromalley.com/. https://www.walteromalley.com/en/biography/short-stops/Planting-the-Education-Seed#:~:text=In%20the%20dedication%20to%20his,sports%20administrators%20need%20academic%20preparation.%E2%80%9D

2
WORKING IN THE SPORT INDUSTRY
The Skills Needed

Introduction

One of the first sport industry job interviews I had was with Madison Square Garden as a sales representative. I had very little sales experience and even less of an interest in sales but was always told, "Sales is your way in the door" thus resulting in an application for the position. Soon after applying, I received a phone call confirming a first-round interview on-site at Madison Square Garden a few weeks later. I was given a one-hour window for the interview and was told to arrive at the start of that hour. A feeling of immense joy was soon followed by a feeling of uncertainty and a lack of preparedness. To prepare for the interview, I focused on learning as much as I could about Madison Square Garden and the products I would be selling tickets for.

The interview day arrived and I was ready to enter Madison Square Garden to proclaim why I would be their next best sales representative. As I entered to check in, a receptionist took my name and instructed me to take a seat in the waiting room. Two things emerged upon entering the waiting room. First was a feeling of accomplishment. Standing in a room covered by photographs of the New York Knicks and New York Rangers provided a sense of "making it." Second was a feeling of familiarity. There were a lot of familiar faces in the waiting room. As I looked around, I recognized a number of classmates from university, all of whom were given the same one-hour time slot to interview for the same exact sales representative position. This was either a very big coincidence or my first realization that obtaining a job within the sport industry was going to be very competitive.

I left the interview unsure of what to expect, and, ultimately, did not get the job. However, I realized something following the interview: The need for differentiation. The majority of us in that waiting room went to the same university and obtained the same degree. So, how do we differentiate ourselves from each other? What skills are needed and, perhaps most importantly, how can these skills be developed?

Skills Needed

The World Economic Forum's Future of Jobs report is a biannual publication that tracks the labor market, highlighting areas of growth and decline, along with trends and disruptions. Its 2023 report surveyed over 800 companies in 45 economic regions of the globe (World Economic Forum, 2023). Within its most recent 2023 report, a section is dedicated to specific skills on the rise. The top five skills identified in this section of the report are below. Those in **bold** are categorized as skills, knowledge, and abilities, while the others are categorized as attitudes.

1. **Creative thinking**
2. **Analytical thinking**
3. **Technological literacy**
4. Curiosity and lifelong learning
5. Resilience, flexibility, and agility

Of the top five identified skills on the rise, there is a mixture presented. Of those identified skills, some would be considered hard skills and some would be considered soft skills (more on these types of skills below). Creative and analytical thinking, numbers one and two above, are the two areas which organizations are focusing on reskilling and upskilling (training initiatives) for their current employees. Over the course of 2023–2027, analytical thinking will account for 10% of all training efforts, whereas creative thinking will account for 8% (World Economic Forum, 2023). Employers are therefore looking for individuals who are well-rounded and possess a variety of qualities which will align with the cultural direction of the organization.

A key to understanding how to best differentiate is to become aware of the skills most desired by employers in the sport industry. You may ask yourself, "Well, how do I do this?" The first step is to begin looking at job advertisements. All job advertisements will include sections related to "Essential Duties/Responsibilities" and "Basic Requirements/Qualifications" within the description of the role. Here you will see the skills and competencies desired and required by the employer for the position being advertised. Presented below is an example. See: Example Job Advertisement: Coordinator of New Sales – NBA

However, before taking a look at the sample job advertisement, it is important to be able to identify two distinct categories of skills: Hard and soft, both of which will be highlighted within the job advertisement itself.

Hard Skills

Hard skills are the skills that are more technical in nature; the skills most identified as teachable skills. For example, accounting, marketing, project management, and foreign languages, among others. These skills, once acquired, are more easily demonstrated and measured (e.g. master's degree with a 4.0 GPA). Hard skills encompass concepts and theories and how to effectively apply those learnings to the workplace. To keep current with changing industry trends, organizations are needing to provide hard skill training to employees. According to Ferreira et al. (2022), companies and organizations typically offer hard skills training to employees in the form of short online courses and through an employee mentorship scheme. These various training initiatives traditionally take place during an onboarding phase, which takes place when an employee first joins the company.

There are a few key concepts which help to define and identify hard skills. First, these skills are **tangible**. Hard skills can be measured and demonstrated more clearly. Second, hard skills are **developed** through learning and application (e.g. education, professional development, employment training). Third, hard skills are **specific** to a job or career, such as obtaining a sport management degree with the aim of working in the sport industry. Fourth, hard skills are **identifiable**. Applicants often fill their resumes and CVs with hard skills as they can clearly align them with the specific requirements for a job advertisement.

Primarily, hard skills have been the focal point of education; as these skills have been identified as needing to be taught. This concept, however, is changing. Hard skills are simply one part of an individual's skill set. Thus, an equally strong emphasis is being placed on soft skills as a part of developing a well-rounded job candidate. This will be elaborated on more in the preceding section.

There were many themes which emerged from the conversations had for this book; however, all of the interviewees placed a strong emphasis on learning, specifically, continued learning. Of the 21 sport industry professionals interviewed, all of them had a bachelor's degree, and all but two had a master's degree. These degrees, in both sport- and non-sport-related disciplines, were imperative to those individuals obtaining the knowledge-base to prepare them for a career in sport; however, the additional learning conducted beyond their university degree helped to separate themselves from their peers.

Certifications and Continuing Professional Development

The Greek philosopher, Plutarch, in his essay on Listening to Lectures stated, "For the mind does not require filling like a bottle, but rather, like wood, it only requires kindling to create in it an impulse to think independently and an ardent desire for the truth" (Ratcliffe, 2017).

Learning does not stop when formalized education has been completed. Lifelong learning is essential for personal and professional growth and development. Learning is continuous and within most fields, essential for keeping up with trends, adapting to change, and staying relevant.

In addition to formalized education, there will be opportunities to continue learning and developing, whether that be in the form of a specific certification or simply a continuing professional development course.

> I've been fortunate enough to enrol myself in and to continue education classes at the two places I've really worked at…when I was at the NBA, they had a Harvard Business program…classes and courses you could take on your own time through Harvard Business School. So, I have a certificate program from that. I did NBA University…where they have the HR (Human Resources) department come in and they go over different things about how to present yourself or write better emails or make sure you've become more well-rounded.
>
> *Alexander Khilnani, Senior Director of Yield Strategy, Revenue Innovation and Analytics, NBC Sports and Olympics*

Depending on your role within the sport industry, continuing education may become more specific to the type of job you have or the department in which you are working. For example, advertising and sales:

> And now at NBC Sports, to the programs I've just recently been involved, which is to, better understand the linear digital landscape and how the

shift in viewership has affected our business. And on this program called LEAP, which is developing the next round of leaders for our ad sales group.

Alexander Khilnani, Senior Director of Yield Strategy, Revenue Innovation and Analytics, NBC Sports and Olympics

Or, as an entrepreneur working to develop sport programs at schools:

We were working with one school that undertook the IB (International Baccalaureate) curriculum. So, they said in order for Sports Pro(company name) to manage our sport program. One of you have to do the IB Sports curriculum. I had to do 500 hours of training with kids and also go through a few tests and exams to be able to get a certification. So, I got a Category 1 certification to be able to teach and support at an IB school.

Rissan Norman, Associate Manager – Intelligence Audience, Wasserman

Or, as a member of the marketing team for a professional football club:

For continuing development, at Aston Villa (I am able to) put myself on courses just for further development. For example, a lot of it is being around women's sport, so learning more about different ways that we could market to more family-based audiences. For example, we were with the FA (Football Association) the other week on a course about how (when marketing tickets) you don't want to go hard on…how much it costs, but more of what there is to experience on the day (at the match).

Jonathan Lock, Marketing Executive, Aston Villa Football Club

Some continued professional development or certifications may be mandatory by the organization you are working for, and others may be the result of your own self-determination to continuously develop and progress. Either way, there are numerous benefits to accepting the path of a lifelong learner. According to McGrath (2023) lifelong learning is driven by curiosity and mastery. Those who are curious have a desire to explore and discover new and useful knowledge. This leads to a mindset of mastery, in which individuals have a desire to develop a level of expertise in their field and reach their full potential.

Continued learning, whether through a certification or voluntary course, can aid in creating new opportunities. Individuals who partake in continued learning will stay ahead within their field, can improve self-confidence, and provide a sense of accomplishment. As we know, sport as an industry is

Language Learning

As sport continues to grow into a global industry, being able to effectively communicate with a variety of stakeholders becomes incredibly important. English may act as a common language within the industry; however, being able to speak another language outside of English will help set you apart and make you more of an attractive candidate to hiring managers.

The ability to speak another language has significant additional benefits. Those who speak another language have greater ease in learning and complex thinking, creativity, communication skills, and interpersonal skills (Academy of Finland, 2009); all of which are soft skills (see below). A 2023 study conducted by Preply highlights that multilingual employees earn an average of 19% more and are 5% more likely to obtain a raise. Perhaps most importantly, however, is that 40% of multilingual employees felt speaking another language helped them to land a job (Mykhalevych, 2023).

How can you get started building your language skills? According to Brower (2023), there are four steps to help you get going. Step one is to simply, begin. Find a class to take, for example, or use a piece of language learning software to get started. The main point is to get going and set small achievable goals. Step two is to commit. Find what works for you in terms of regular learning and create a schedule which you can stick to. Step three is immersion. This can be quite difficult if you are not surrounded by the language you are learning to speak often. However, this can be easily fixed by watching a television show or movie in the desired language or finding a local community of speakers practicing the language. Finally, step four is to stay motivated. Why do you want to learn another language? What benefits will this provide? Think about what will inspire you and keep you motivated to staying on track in your efforts to learn another language.

> Once I finished my masters…I did a lot of language courses. I was really open to any experience I could have. I preferred going outside of the UK, rather to Europe. And this is what motivated me to learn languages. And for example, with Spanish, I developed it in Spain when I did a year abroad there. I have used it so many times at events, recently at the world championships in Spain.
>
> *Timotej Dudas, Event and Project Manager,*
> *The International Ski and Snowboard*
> *Federation (FIS)*

From my current role, languages are very necessary, you know? I had the opportunity of growing up in Switzerland. So, I spoke French, English and I had kind of learned Spanish prior to university. And then I perfected it after my education, so that would be one piece of advice. It's free to go and use Duolingo and at least have a base level knowledge of a language. And I would say specifically Spanish if it's the USA. But a language that is needed in a country or region where a person is interested in in working in.

Theren Bullock, Foundation Senior Manager,
Fédération Internationale de Basketball (FIBA)

Soft Skills

When thinking of soft skills, typically, one thinks of communication, empathy, listening, adaptability, working in a team, and/or leadership. Traditionally, soft skills have been thought of as skills that are continuously developed and acquired, more so than taught. According to entrepreneur and leadership expert, Rachel Wells, soft skills are classified as human-centered skills which are transferable, non-technical, and intangible (Wells, 2024). Soft skills, or interpersonal skills, are the personal qualities and traits which are needed for effective communication, peer collaboration, and general success within social settings.

There are a few key concepts which help to define and identify soft skills. First, soft skills are **interactive and personal**. These skills focus on relationship-building, exchange, communication, empathy, and listening. Second, soft skills are **specific** to a career in the sport industry. Employers strongly value the ability to effectively communicate, empathize, and work together. Third, soft skills are **adaptable**. These skills can be used in a variety of situations and applied to a variety of contexts. Fourth, soft skills are **continuous**. These skills can and should be developed over time.

From an employer perspective, soft skills are full of value. Soft skills allow for employees to more easily become a part of a cohesive unit and team within an organization. Soft skills aid in contributing towards a positive working environment, one of teamwork and communication. Since 2020 the need for soft skills and organizational soft skill training increased. Soft skills started to become a major focus in company culture and workplace environment (Ferreira et al., 2022). Specifically, communication, as the act of communication aids in internal (e.g. team meetings) and external (e.g. interacting with clients) workings. Further, during conversations with those sport industry professionals in leadership positions, all viewed the ability to effectively communicate as vital to success in their role. Therefore, there should be a strong emphasis on the development of soft skills and the ability to highlight and demonstrate those specific skills to employers.

Preparation or the ability to prepare was a central theme amongst those interviewed for this book.

> Everyone wants things easy, especially now more than ever, and sometimes it takes a little bit more time for yourself to be over prepared. We just expect certain things to happen to us and that's the wrong attitude to have, I believe.
>
> *Theren Bullock, Foundation Senior Manager,*
> *Fédération Internationale de Basketball*
> *(FIBA)*

When asked how one can approach an interview or conversation with a sport organization confidently, the answer fell around over preparation.

> It's being over prepared. It's being a master of your craft. It is amazing to me how unprepared people come to interviews. Basic things, such as mission and vision, but also just read the last five articles the organization has released.
>
> *Theren Bullock, Foundation Senior Manager,*
> *Fédération Internationale de Basketball*
> *(FIBA)*

Communication

Regardless of the role you have, communication skills are necessary to work in the sport industry. In order to communicate effectively, however, you must understand how to communicate. Communication, on a basic level, is comprised of two parts: Verbal and non-verbal. Verbal communication is simply the act of transferring thought into words. Non-verbal communication, in contrast, is where an individual expresses thought through body language or gestures. Effective communication in the sport industry goes beyond being able to engage with colleagues while in the work place. Communication expands from the internal working environment and into the external working world of your organization. For example, take the organization you currently work for, or aspire to work for and identify who that organization interacts with on a daily basis. Who are its key stakeholders? How often is the organization communicating with those stakeholders?

> ...I've developed some of the skills that have allowed me to be successful in the sports industry.

Stubborn, honest, **direct communicator** but also thrive in a team environment.

Beth Porreca, Managing Director High Performance and National Teams, USA Football

I really had my critical thinking and writing skills, which now I use on daily basis at my work…I learned, how to communicate. I learned how to how to engage with people.

Timotej Dudas, Event and Project Manager, The International Ski and Snowboard Federation (FIS)

According to Emerson (2021), "A leader's ability to communicate clearly and effectively with employees, within teams, and across the organization is one of the foundations of a successful business." In today's advancing world, with new technology and ways to communicate constantly on the horizon, communication ability is one of the most critical skills a manager should have. In order to maximize your communication potential, Emerson (2021) further encourages communication to be clear, concise, and prepared in advance. In order to do this, you need to understand who you are communicating to and what their expectations may be. Finally, do not forget about the tone in which you are conversing or relaying through and the importance of non-verbal communication, which can carry significantly higher impact than spoken word (Smith, 2013).

To look at this from an industry perspective, let's take a look at Sportfive as a quick example. Sportfive is an international sport marketing agency with over 50 offices around the world, and clients representing over 30 sports, such as the Los Angeles Lakers and Borussia Dortmund (Sportfive, 2024). Despite the ever-changing environment around the sport industry, one constant remains the focal point of Sportfive: People.

Sportfive is one of the largest and biggest sport marketing agencies in the world. What we do, we work with two sides in the value chain of the sports economy: rights' holders, such as an athlete, the NFL, the European Football Club, or in my case, the International Handball Federation…We do work with brands (the other side), with corporate brands who are using the platform of sport to communicate and to set up their marketing plans to achieve their corporate objectives, such as, awareness, image transfer…

Ole Schilke, Executive Director, Sportfive

From a marketing perspective, people are consumers who are at the core of any marketing campaign and initiative. Therefore, according to Dominic Mills (2023) of Sportfive, communication plays a critical role in all their marketing functions. Communication is a tool which helps to understand and inform a targeted audience, clientele, and coworkers. Further, the marketers themselves need to interact with potential consumers in a particular way. They need to know how to best communicate (e.g. most effective communication channels) with consumers and stakeholders. Further, Sportfive's collaborative efforts are based significantly around open communication.

Interpersonal Skills

The blend of communication skills and people skills can be referred to as interpersonal skills. As the sport industry is one of engagement and relationships, a strong mix of communication skills and people skills is needed. Interpersonal skills are identified as soft skills, and therefore there is a stigma around this type of skill being attributed to simply being a people person, or not.

However, interpersonal skills, despite not being taught per se as a hard skill, can very much be learned and developed. These skills can be complex, as the combination of communication and people skills encompass a range of behaviors and attitudes, which contribute to successful communication and collaboration with others. Interpersonal skills are utilized in effectively interacting with others in a variety of social settings. These skills are necessary for building and maintaining relationships. Alex Strafer, an Account Executive of Group Sales with DC United of Major League Soccer (MLS), highlights one of his key priorities as building relationships with clients each day.

> …if it helps you create a little bit of a relationship that drives more tickets, go out and do it…Grow the relationship with the person.

At this point you should have a better understanding of communication skills in general and their importance through reading this chapter thus far. Beyond communicating well, a key component of interpersonal skills is empathy. Empathy is the ability to connect with others through the understanding of feelings in a way which demonstrates care or concern. Being empathetic towards others can lead to developing stronger relationships; whether that be with colleagues or clients.

Collaboration is also a major component within the realm of interpersonal skills. Sport is a collaborative industry, and whether you are a coach working with players, an account executive selling tickets to fans, or a marketer pitching sponsorship proposals to brands, working together is key.

Collaboration includes the contribution of ideas, working in teams, compromising, and, at times, resolving conflict. Navigating the various avenues of interpersonal skills can strengthen a working environment and help aid in achieving common goals and objectives.

A part of interpersonal skills also includes being socially and culturally aware. Cultural competence recognizes and values diverse cultures and identifies within society. This includes understanding, learning from, and valuing all members of society. As the sport industry is increasing its global presence this becomes even more applicable for those looking to work in sport.

Interpersonal skills are a key foundational piece towards successful relationship building and overall daily interaction. Developing these skills will enhance your employability within the industry and help to put you on the path towards being successful in and out of sport.

Hard and Soft Skills: Working Together

Despite the identifiable differences between hard and soft skills, these sets of skills should work in conjunction with each other. Research conducted by Lamri and Lubart (2023) find hard and soft skills should be complementary of each other. Both sets of skills are easily classified separately, yet a strong understanding of the interdependence between the two can help to develop a more comprehensive skill set. Therefore, as one goes about developing the skills necessary to embark on a career in the sport industry, it should be with a plethora of skills, both hard and soft. Hard skills, may in effect, get you an interview; however, it will be the soft skills which ultimately land you the job.

The knowledge in which you have learned or obtained, as a hard skill, can only be enhanced by developed soft skills. One can go to university to learn about working in the sport industry and can learn the concepts needed to be applied within a business setting. Thus, preparing themselves with a knowledge base suitable for employment in the industry. However, it is one thing to learn the concepts and theory around sales, management, or marketing and another thing to convey and apply those learned concepts. Through developed and useable soft skills, those working in the sport industry combine the concepts and theories they have learned with communication, leadership, creativity, etc. to become more effective in their role.

Strategically, both hard and soft skills are needed in combination to not only get an interview and demonstrate the skills needed for the job but to also advance in your career through relationship building, promotions, pay raises, and career direction changes (Wells, 2024). A combination and understanding of a variety of skills will be most beneficial for a sport-related career. As Wei and Sotiriadou (2023) state, those who pursue a profession in sport find themselves undertaking two distinct career avenues: Boundaryless and protean (Minten & Forsyth, 2014). The first is a career which spans movement across job roles, organizations, and industries. And the second is a career driven by one's values and motivations. Regardless of the avenue taken and the reasons behind changing jobs, a generic set of relevant hard and soft skills are needed for continuous employability throughout the duration of a career.

Therefore, as Lussier and Kimball (2023) state, those looking to work in leadership or management roles in sport need to have well defined management skills. The authors define management skills as skills inclusive of technical skills (hard skills), people skills, communication skills, conceptual skills, and decision-making skills (all soft skills). These skills are utilized in conjunction with each other. Those hard skills are needed to perform technical tasks, such as operating customer relationship management (CRM) software for ticket sales executives. While the soft skills enable you to work well with others, to communicate messages clearly and effectively, in a sponsorship proposal for example, to conceptualize ideas through elements of thinking critically, and to make decisions to solve problems. The more well-rounded a skill set you possess, the more marketable and beneficial you become to sport industry organizations.

Degrees and Higher Education

A recommended starting point to obtain, combine, and develop hard and soft skills is through formalized education, specifically, higher education. Higher education globally is focusing on providing well-rounded education opportunities to students. Therefore, much emphasis is placed on teaching knowledge and content while also focusing on critical thinking, communication, interpersonal skills, and creativity, amongst others. Therefore, investing in a higher education degree will not only provide you with a necessary qualification to apply for a job but also the starting point for acquiring and developing a wide range of hard and soft skills.

As you will see with the job posting below, a higher education degree (e.g. bachelor's) is expected. Further, many of these positions will also encourage or find desirable a master's degree. It is not necessary to obtain solely a sport-related degree, as general business, management, marketing, or policy degrees will teach you same theories and principles. However, sport-related degrees will provide the context of sport and apply those general theories and principles through a sport-specific lens.

Starting out as an academic discipline, sport-related higher education programs focusing on the business of sport were identified as either Sport Management or Sport Administration. Over the years, however, niche or more focused programs have been created. Sport Analytics (e.g. Syracuse University, USA), Sustainable Sport Business (e.g. Loughborough University

London, UK), Sport Policy and Governance (e.g. Manchester Metropolitan University, UK), Sports Leadership (e.g. Northeastern University, USA), or Management, Law and Humanities of Sport (e.g. FIFA International Masters, UK, Italy, Switzerland), among others, have entered the field. Depending on the route you would like to take working in the sport industry, you may look to take on a more general sport-related program, or a more focused sport-related program.

Example Job Advertisement: Coordinator of New Sales – NBA

Below you will see part of a job advertisement for a previously advertised sales position with a National Basketball Association (NBA) club. This position was posted on www.teamworkonline.com during the month of September 2023 (TeamWork Online, 2023). The desired and required skills for the position have been separated into "Basic Requirements/Qualifications" in Table 2.1 and "Essential Duties/Responsibilities" in Table 2.2.

What do you notice when reading through the job description? What hard skills, or soft skills, appear? When reading through the sample job description you will notice some keywords or phrases in **bold**, underlined, or **both**. This has been done to help identify both the hard and soft skills being asked for. In bold are the **hard skills** and underlined are the soft skills.

TABLE 2.1 Basic Requirements and Qualifications

Basic Requirements/Qualifications:
- Open to any qualified applicant who can meet the time commitment and has a recent **college degree**, Bachelors or Masters.
- The ability to work flexible hours to include nights, weekends and holidays is required
- **Proficiency in Microsoft Office programs** required
- The ideal candidate should have an expert background in **video editing**, and a **portfolio that demonstrates the ability to deliver engaging work**
- **Proficient in Adobe Premiere Pro, iMovie Final Cut Pro, Adobe Photoshop, Event Photography**
- Story-driven **editing and producing** experience
- Demonstrated organizational and time management skills and works well under deadline pressure
- Must be organized, creative, enthusiastic, and possess excellent interpersonal skills
- Must be able to handle multiple jobs simultaneously and work well under pressure
- **Proficiency in Archtics and Salesforce** preferred

TABLE 2.2 Essential Duties and Responsibilities

Essential Duties/Responsibilities:

- Complete **various sales reports** on a daily, weekly and monthly basis
- **Research and analyze market trends** for prospecting opportunities
- Assist other ticket sales departments with projects as they arise
- Assist with game night responsibilities for revenue generating or retention events
- Help <u>create content</u> and short posts for sales managers and reps
- <u>**Understand calendar of events**</u> for the week, and know where you need to be for each to capture video/content
- <u>**Develop recruiting and training**</u> videos for Inside Sales

---

Those which are both in **<u>bold and underlined</u>** are asking for a combination of skills.

Conclusion

The sport industry is a competitive landscape. Its popularity and excitement as an industry make it a desirable career choice. This only enhances the need for those looking to embark on a career in sport. However, it is important to fully understand the ins and outs of the industry prior to deciding on it as a career path. Once you have made the decision to go all in on a career in sport you need to be able to pull away from the pack and differentiate yourself from your peers. In order to best do this, you need to fully understand the skills required to work in the industry and the job roles you are interested in taking. As you search and apply for available jobs, focus on the hard and soft skills which are most desirable. Compare those needed skills to the skills you currently possess, keeping in mind that you will only continue to develop your skill set as you go along your career. In the final chapter, Chapter 7, you will focus on taking the skills you possess and articulating them on your resume (CV) and cover letter.

Action Item 2: What Skills Do You Need to Develop?

With Action Item 1 you were asked to identify five different areas of the sport industry you were interested in and rank them according to personal importance. For Action Item 2 you are to now build upon that initial table by identifying the specific skills, both hard and soft, needed to work in those respective areas, as well as a brief developmental plan for obtaining those skills. See the example below in the first row of Table 2.3 of a Player

TABLE 2.3 Action Item 2

Sport Business Area	Specific Job	Hard Skills	Soft Skills	Developmental Plan
*Player Development	Tennis Administrator	Bachelor's Degree. English speaking mandatory, Spanish speaking a plus.	Interpersonal Skills. Strong communicator: both oral and written.	Finish bachelor's degree; take a leading role in classroom discussions. Download Duolingo and begin Spanish lessons.

*Example

Development Tennis Administrator and then begin to fill out the rest of the table with your own specifics for each of the five identified job roles.

Further Resources

Coursera. https://www.coursera.org/
The reader can learn and develop new skills through online learning courses. Many of the university collaborated courses provided are free.
Duolingo. https://www.duolingo.com/
A free online and app-based language learning resource. The reader can get a jump start on developing a new language skill.
TeamWork Online. https://www.teamworkonline.com/
The reader can benefit from using TeamWork Online as it is one of the larger sport and entertainment online job boards. Search for and apply for jobs in the industry directly through their website.

References

Academy of Finland. (2009, October 9). *Brains benefit from multilingualism*. ScienceDaily. https://www.sciencedaily.com/releases/2009/10/091029151807.htm
Brower, T. (2023, October 1). Improve your salary and career by speaking a second language. *Forbes*. https://www.forbes.com/sites/tracybrower/2023/10/01/improve-your-salary-and-career-by-speaking-a-second-language/?sh=7b9d7c6c7497
Emerson, M. (2021, August 30). *8 ways you can improve your communication skills – Professional & executive development | Harvard DCE*. Professional & Executive Development | Harvard DCE. https://professional.dce.harvard.edu/blog/8-ways-you-can-improve-your-communication-skills/
Ferreira, C., Robertson, J., & Pitt, L. (2022). Business (un)usual: Critical skills for the next normal. *Thunderbird International Business Review*, 65(1), 39–47. https://doi.org/10.1002/tie.22276
Lamri, J., & Lubart, T. (2023). Reconciling hard skills and soft skills in a common framework: The generic skills component approach. *Journal of Intelligence*, 11(6), 107. https://doi.org/10.3390/jintelligence11060107
Lussier, R. N., & Kimball, D. C. (2023). *Applied sport management skills*. Human Kinetics.
McGrath, R. (2023, April 25). The power of lifelong learning: How curiosity forges mastery. *Forbes*. https://www.forbes.com/sites/forbesbusinesscouncil/2023/04/21/the-power-of-lifelong-learning-how-curiosity-forges-mastery/
Mills, D. (2023, January 11). *Sports marketing careers: Winning with soft skills*. SPORTFIVE – Sportsmarketing Agency. https://sportfive.co.uk/beyond-the-match/insights/careers-in-sports-marketing-how-soft-skills-help-you-win-big
Minten, S. R., & Forsyth, J. (2014). The careers of sports graduates: Implications for employability strategies in higher education sports courses. *Journal of Hospitality, Leisure, Sport & Tourism Education*, 15, 94–102. https://doi.org/10.1016/j.jhlste.2014.06.004
Mykhalevych, N. (2023, October 25). Highest paying cities for multilingual employees – Preply. *Language Learning with Preply Blog*. https://preply.com/en/blog/highest-paying-cities-for-multilingual-workers/
Ratcliffe, S. (2017). *Oxford essential quotations* (5th ed.). Oxford University Press. https://doi.org/10.1093/acref/9780191843730.001.0001

Smith, J. (2013, March 11). 10 nonverbal cues that convey confidence at work. *Forbes.* https://www.forbes.com/sites/jacquelynsmith/2013/03/11/10-nonverbal-cues-that-convey-confidence-at-work/?sh=690675fe5e13

Sportfive. (2024). *SPORTFIVE – Sports marketing agency.* SPORTFIVE Global Holding GmbH. https://sportfive.com/

TeamWork Online. (2023, September). Coordinator, new sales – Atlanta Hawks. https://www.teamworkonline.com/basketball-jobs/atlanta-hawks-jobs/atlanta-hawks-jobs/coordinator-new-sales-2054494

Wei, R., & Sotiriadou, P. (2023). Teaching generic skill sets to sport undergraduates to increase their employability and promote smooth college-to-work transition. *Journal of Hospitality, Leisure, Sport & Tourism Education, 32,* 100431. https://doi.org/10.1016/j.jhlste.2023.100431

Wells, R. (2024, February 19). Soft skills vs. power skills – Is there a difference? *Forbes.* https://www.forbes.com/sites/rachelwells/2024/02/19/soft-skills-vs-power-skills-is-there-a-difference/?sh=4a498ac168a0

World Economic Forum. (2023, December 21). *The future of jobs report 2023.* https://www.weforum.org/publications/the-future-of-jobs-report-2023/

3
WHY DO YOU WANT TO WORK IN THE SPORT INDUSTRY?

Introduction

The process of identifying a career, in general, is a daunting task for anyone, let alone a career in the sport industry. There are numerous avenues one can take, as highlighted in Chapter 1, and as you will read in Chapter 4, the path to obtaining that career is not always linear. Therefore, to put yourself in the best position to obtain an interview and to be a competitive prospect

DOI: 10.4324/9781003389330-3

for a job opportunity, you need to be able to convey why you want to work in this industry in the first place. What about the sport industry is appealing to you? What separates working in this industry from a career outside of sport?

As an initial starting point, take a moment for self-reflection. What do you think are your strengths, and how do those strengths fit into the sport industry? Not only will you feel more comfortable in your role, but utilizing your strengths at work also leads to a better quality of life and higher levels of engagement and productivity (Flade et al., 2015). Take a moment to list some of your strengths in Table 3.1 below.

TABLE 3.1 My Strengths

My Strengths
–
–
–
–
–
–
–

Action Item 3: My Strengths

Those interviewed for this book, like many, participated in sport at some level for a period of their life. There was already an established connection to the sport industry, and therefore an identification that sport could lead to a career. This is not to suggest that one must be an athlete to work in sport but instead to showcase an identifiable starting point for why. The interviewees all had and have a passion for sport.

> I did realize at some point that I wanted to escape the world of sports. But at the same time, realizing that when trying other things, I also realize that… (with sport) I can see myself spending 10 hours a day working on it because this is what I know the best and this is also where my interest is.
>
> *Valentin Capelli, Manager Sport Movement Relations, World Anti-Doping Agency (WADA)*

Regardless of your experience as an athlete or non-athlete, you should have your own identifiable reasons for pursuing a career in this industry. In addition to the identified strengths above, what are your values and passions? More on values and passions later in this chapter. However, similar to listing your strengths above, in Table 3.2 below, write out some of your values and passions. For passions, what motivates you; what gets you up in the morning? *I am passionate about helping people and solving problems creatively.* For values, what is important to you? *I value collaborative working and a team environment.*

TABLE 3.2 My Values and Passions

My Values	My Passions
–	–
–	–
–	–
–	–
–	–

Action Item 4: My Values and Passions

> I tried to see where I could do the best….achieve the best because of my background (in sport) and also at the same time what was the most interesting. So, it's a combination.
> *Valentin Capelli, Manager Sport Movement Relations, World Anti-Doping Agency (WADA)*

Career consultant, Dr Kyle Elliott (2023), emphasizes finding your career North Star as you identify a prospective career avenue. Simply put, what does your career big picture look like? As you embark on a career in the sport industry, it may seem like a difficult task to project your short- and long-term goals as you are still considering which aspect of the industry is appealing, and what types of jobs exist within that aspect of sport. However, having some direction and aspiration for where you would like your career to go is beneficial. It may seem a bit cliché, but you will likely be on the receiving end of the "Where do you see yourself in five years?" question at some point in your career. Therefore, have you thought of any short-term and long-term goals you may have and if so, how do these goals align with a career in the sport industry? Below in Table 3.3, begin to write down three short-term and three long-term career goals.

TABLE 3.3 Short- and Long-Term Goals

Short-Term Goals	Long-Term Goals
–	–
–	–
–	–
–	–
–	–

Action Item 5: Short- and Long-Term Goals

As this chapter concludes, you will have the opportunity to put all of this together, but for the time being, you have started the process of understanding who you are, what you identify as your strengths, what you value, what you are passionate about, and what you want to start accomplishing in your career. Now, let's transition focus to the sport industry to better understand why this industry is being considered as the desired industry of choice. Why sport and what is it like to actually work there?

Understanding the "Why?"

> I think working in sports...it has to be your passion. It has to be something you love.
>
> *Karina Klein, Senior Manager Coach and Player Services / Junior Tennis, United States Tennis Association (USTA)*

To begin thinking about your journey towards working in the sport industry, ask yourself the question: Why? Why do I want to work in this industry, specifically? What about the sport industry is attractive, interesting, or appealing to me? Ultimately, the answer to this question will drive your journey forward and provide you with clarity during the process.

As discussed in Chapter 1, the industry of sport in itself is exciting, highly publicized, and profitable. The current value of the global sport market is $512 billion, with this number expected to grow to $624 billion by 2027 (Statista, 2023). As Weight et al. (2021) highlights, a significant number of younger professionals are drawn to the sport industry as it is a career path that most closely aligns with their fandom, while also being in an exciting and, at times, celebrity-filled industry. However, it is important to understand that those working in the sport industry are all contributing to making sport the way it is. Each role plays an intricate part and not all experiences of working in the industry are that of professional athletes, celebrities, and fandom.

> It's not all glamorous, but the process can be really fulfilling and a lot of fun. And so, if you are into the work, the daily grind; taking those small steps of getting better – then it can be fulfilling. If you are just looking for that moment to take your picture with the trophy or the ring ceremony, I think you are probably in it for the wrong reasons.
>
> *Dr Larry Lauer, Mental Skills Coach, United States Tennis Association (USTA)*

There are only so many "glamorous" professional head coaching or general manager opportunities available. However, these "highly desired" positions only play a small part in the overall operation of the industry. There are numerous dedicated behind the scenes individuals tasked with ensuring the industry continues to operate as a success, those working in marketing, for example. A needed group, tasked with creating awareness through promotion, with a desired result of getting you in the door and hooked on their product. Marketing, within the sport industry, drives elements of fan engagement and organizational branding, while also aiding in revenue-generating activities such as ticket sales, sponsorships, and partnerships. Ultimately, marketing plays an integral role in connecting a sport organization with its target audience, generating revenue and maintaining a brand presence. Without those working in marketing, amongst many others, the sport industry would not be the industry it is today.

Insights from Those Working in the Industry

Understanding what it is truly like to work in the sport industry will only come with personal experience. As you study the business of sport, you will obtain glimpses into the inner workings of the industry and from that be able to derive your own insights into the various working components of the sport industry. However, until you begin your career and obtain your own experiences, you can best learn about what it is like to work in the sport industry now from those who are currently doing it on a day to day basis. Below are a few quotes which provide a starting point for insight into what it is actually like working in the sport industry:

> Daunting, fast moving, vibrant and interesting place to work. Not for the faint of heart. Dynamic, fascinating, time hungry, so difficult to have a

balanced life. Ultimately, I would certainly not say anything bad about it. It's been a fantastic journey.

Anonymous, Chief Executive Officer

The sports industry is magnificent. Working within the sport industry… you have to keep on learning something new, something innovative.

Harsh Khandwala, Sponsorship Executive, Percept Ltd

It's a lot of work and it's not your 9 to 5 job. It's more because sports are not happening from 9 to 5 during the week. It's always night. And then on the weekends and so it does, I would say require a special motivation to be willing to do that and to sacrifice a lot of time and my feeling so far is that it's not very, hasn't been very high paid. So, I feel like for me, you need to find that level of I'm actually working with something that I enjoy and that I'm interested in versus the monetary benefits that comes out of it. So, I feel like these are the things that you should consider when thinking about going into the sporting industry.

Torill Lunde, Business Development Manager, Joymo

Chapter 7 will provide you with the thoughts of all those interviewed on what they have learned thus far along their journey. Speaking with those interviewed for this book, two themes emerged around working in the industry: Understanding what the job actually entails and understanding the expectations and misconceptions of working in sport.

Understand What the Job Entails

As you begin to establish your "why" for working in the sport industry, it is necessary to best understand what the job itself is going to entail. In the quotes above, Torill highlights the need to work outside of normal business hours, while the anonymous Chief Executive Officer describes the industry's fast-moving environment and the difficulty of having a balanced life. Therefore, it is strongly recommended to understand what the career you are striving for entails and to ensure you want to work in an industry which operates differently from other industries.

To begin, research. Seek to find out as much as you can about what specific jobs require and expect. You can easily start this process by reading through the duties and responsibilities of roles you are interested in. This will at least provide a glimpse into what you will be doing on a daily basis. Many times, when a hiring manager has posted a job, on LinkedIn for example, there is a call for interested candidates to reach out to either discuss the position or to ask any questions they may have about the position itself. This is a perfect opportunity to not only express an interest and demonstrate motivation but simply learn more about the job and the expectations of the organization.

There are a variety of job roles and avenues you can have within the industry; however, despite the varying and numerous career choices available, there are specific expectations and some misconceptions which are applicable to those careers. A part of understanding what it will be like to work in the sport industry is to understand what is expected of you as an employee, and what misconceptions there are associated with working in the industry. There are four key expectations and misconceptions listed below. This should not be viewed as an exhaustive list, as different individuals in the industry will have differing opinions and viewpoints. However, from those interviewed, these four emerged as important for someone unfamiliar with the industry and looking to have a career within it.

Expectation and Misconceptions

1. **Working Hours:** Working in the sport industry will not be Monday to Friday from 9:00 am to 5:00 pm. There are a variety of avenues and career paths one can take in the industry, and therefore more of a traditional working schedule may exist for some roles. However, for the majority, and for those interviewed for this book, it is likely your job role will take you beyond Monday to Friday from 9:00 am to 5:00 pm. There will be instances where you will work outside of the traditional working hours, especially if you are working with a team or athletes. This does not mean you will always have to work additional hours, but instead of beginning at 9:00 am, you may begin your day at 12:00 pm, and then work into the evening (e.g. game day).

Working in sport requires flexible working hours. In Chapter 2, you explored a previously posted job description to identify and analyze the various soft and hard skill requirements. If you take another look at this job description, you will find the following statement under "Essential Duties/Responsibilities": *Assist with game night responsibilities for revenue generating or retention events.* There is an expectation that your working hours will go beyond the typical 9:00 am to 5:00 pm and spill over into evenings, weekends, and holidays.

> It is different from what you would think from the outside…you will get some very cool experiences, but you have to work very hard. Working for a Premier League football team is seven days a week. You have got to be available. You have got to be on the ball.
>
> *Jonathan Lock, Marketing Executive, Aston Villa Football Club*

2. **Being a Former Athlete:** You do not need to be a former elite athlete to have a successful career in the sport industry. Participation in sport, at any level, is not a prerequisite to working in the industry. Of course, former athletes do work in the industry; however, this is not a requirement or expectation. More so, you will find those working in the industry have a passion to be in and around sport. Of those interviewed for this book, only one played sport, briefly, at a professional level. The majority of the rest played at a recreational or competitive level; youth, high school, or collegiate sport.
3. **Salary:** As an entry-level employee, you, most likely, will not have a high salary. Compensation, especially for an entry-level position, can be lower than other industries. In regard to salary and pay:

> Starting out, you're not going to make a lot of money.
> *Elise Cloutier, Marketing, Youth Program and Business Development Director for Liverpool Football Club International Academies*

> I would say it's a competitive marketplace....comparatively, you're not going to be paid as much as some of the Fortune 500 companies are paying. So, I mean you could be a lawyer for example and you could go work at a law firm and you would probably make three times what you make as a general counsel for a pro team.
> *Beth Porreca, Managing Director High Performance and National Teams, USA Football*

> Do not look at the money and rather look at what is it in sport that you actually want to do.
> *Rissan Norman, Associate Manager – Intelligence & Audience, Wasserman*

There are a lot of people who want to work in the industry all of whom are qualified and many of whom are even over-qualified. This type of demand increases the competitive nature of sport employment, thus opening the door for sport organizations to pay lower salaries in comparison to other industries, while having unpaid internships readily available (Wong, 2008). Therefore, go into entry-level positions with the expectation to be paid a bit less than your peers working in other industries. With that, keep in mind your salary is not a direct determinant of your skills and value, especially with entry-level roles. You are playing a vital role in the delivery of sport, while also working in an industry in which you are truly passionate about!

4. **Recognition:** Much of the work done on a daily basis is done behind the scenes. Therefore, recognition is limited in the eyes of those viewing sport from the outside.

At times it may seem as though working in sport is a thankless job, or at the very least, you may perceive it as such. All of the behind the scenes work that goes into ensuring an event is successful, or that a facility operates to its potential each day, often goes unnoticed, or is simply overlooked by the wider consumer or fan. However, public recognition should not be the main reason for working in the industry. Those interviewed for this book all echoed a similar sentiment around their overall enjoyment for their work. Despite any type of public recognition, each day they felt as though their job was unique and they could not envision working in another industry.

> It's not easy, but I think if you if it's truly your passion, I think it's just an amazing field to be in and there's so many options…I mean, it's pretty amazing when you truly think of all the options in sports.
> Karina Klein, Senior Manager Coach and Player Services / Junior Tennis, United States Tennis Association (USTA)

Find Your Passion

Over the course of an 11-year period, Dobrow Riza and Heller (2015) researched the differences between intrinsic (e.g. industry I am happy to work in) and extrinsic (e.g. job security, high pay) motivators as predictors for career choices and successes in young musicians. The study followed a number of people who aspired to have careers in the music industry. Their research focused on the decision-making of those individuals to better understand what motivated them to either pursue a career in the music industry or not. The authors found that those who prioritized intrinsic motivators and choose to, as the title of the research eludes, "follow their heart" were more likely to end up in a career in which they passioned. Further, their research led to the belief that extrinsic motivators, like salary, were less important compared to that of intrinsic motivators, such as passion and desire. Despite the research study being conducted around aspiring musicians, the key takeaways are very much applicable to the motivators behind working in the sport industry. Those who were interviewed for this book found their way to a career in the sport industry through intrinsic motivators: Happiness, values, and passion.

There is a common saying amongst many giving advice to those entering the job market for the first time: "follow your passion." It can be assumed that by reading this book and showcasing an interest in working in the sport industry, you have a passion for sport. But, what aspect of the sport industry are you passionate about? How do you know you have found your passion?

Sociologist and author, Dr Tracy Brower, suggests focusing on your thoughts and feelings to determine your passion. What about the sport industry makes you interested and curious? What area do you want to learn more about, or want to explore further? Do you notice a specific soft skill (refer back to Chapter 2) which you find yourself good at? The answers to these questions signify identified passion.

Let's use the example of working in ticket sales for a sport organization. Those individuals set goals to reach ticket sales quotas and to, ultimately, fill a stadium. However, their passion lies beyond simply selling tickets and falls more so within communication and the human connection. Talking with clients and getting to know them on a more personal level to understand their needs and wants, while looking to provide unique and entertaining experiences to meet the needs of those clients.

Alex Strafer, an Account Executive in Group Sales with DC United of Major Leaguer Soccer (MLS), is in the business of selling tickets, but he may argue it is more so in the business of formulating and building relationships. As he points out, relationship building is not only a necessary starting point with prospective clients, but it is also the part of his job he is most passionate about.

> I always say you are never going to trust a stranger with your credit card at the end of the day. So, (before jumping into sales mode) I want to know how many kids you have, where you went to college, and work that into the first 10 minutes of our conversation. Finding out what works and what does not work with them…that is really where I just grew into loving what I do.
> *Alex Strafer, Account Executive Group Sales,*
> *DC United*

Your identified passion should align with a heightened sense of emotion and excitement. Simply put, you should feel energized about the prospective of the opportunity or of the role itself. In addition, you should have an innate curiosity and desire to learn more about the aspect of the sport industry you are leaning towards working in. While exploring a prospective career avenue within the sport industry are you genuinely enthusiastic about it? Will it provide you with a sense of purpose?

...it's not (always) glamorous, but the process can be really fulfilling and a lot of fun.

Dr Larry Lauer, Director of Mental Performance, United States Tennis Association (USTA)

Action Item 6: Why a Career in This Industry?

Are you ready to answer the question of "why?" For Action Item 6 you are to continue building upon your journey to working in the sport industry by focusing on the real reasons for why you want to work in the sport industry in the first place. Below, in Table 3.4, are four boxes for you to complete. You will see an example in *italics* at the top of each of the four boxes.

TABLE 3.4 Answering the "Why?"

First: Why the sport industry?	Second: What is my passion?
*Sport has been a continuous part of my life from an early age. I may not be able to be a professional athlete; however, I can still be a part of the industry and have a successful career within sport. **Example*	*I am passionate about helping people and solving problems creatively. I have a passion for the sport of tennis and I would like to work in a role which allows me the opportunity to work directly with athletes and coaches.*
Third: A sport job which aligns with your passion	Fourth: What does the job entail?
A tennis administrator working directly with athletes and coaches. This is not a coaching specific job; however, I would still be working with and around athletes and coaches. My number one choice from Chapter 1.	*Provide administrative support; manage data; collaborative and interpersonal skills; knowledge of professional tennis; excellent communicator.*

The first is simply your reasons for why. What drives your desire to work in this industry? Why sport over other industries (especially those which may provide you higher pay and more consistent hours)? Think about what motivates your decision to work in the sport industry. Is it because of intrinsic or extrinsic motivators? **The second** focuses on your passion. This does not have to be sport related, but in general, what are you passionate about? **The third** box asks for you to find a job in sport which aligns with your identified passion. This could be one of the jobs from Chapter 1, or it could be a new job entirely. Why are you passionate about this aspect of the sport industry? Finally, **the fourth** box asks you to describe what the job, from the third box, actually entails. You may want to do a quick search online for this type of job and take a look at the essential duties and responsibilities (refer back to Chapter 2). How do the essential duties and responsibilities align with your passions?

Conclusion

Why do you want to work in the sport industry? Can you answer that question more clearly now? Your desire to work in the sport industry should be easily conveyed and articulated should you be asked the "why?" question. This may be during an interview or written within a cover letter. The sport industry is one which can be glamorous; however, those working in the industry have a distinct passion for sport. Not all career paths in the industry lead to working in professional sport and elite athletes. Many sport industry careers are behind the scenes, keeping the sport industry operating on a continuously growing and global level. As a career, specifically at the entry-level stage, the hours are long and the salary is low. You will likely experience your peers, outside of the sport industry, working different hours from yourself and receiving a different salary. Keep focus on your intrinsic motivators for wanting to work in sport in the first place. Your rationale for wanting to work in this industry should be clear. Remember, embarking on a career in the sport industry requires a specific mindset; one which showcases you are in it for the right reasons.

Further Resources

Brower, T., PhD. (2022, July 4). Follow your passion really is good advice: 3 ways to fuel your career. *Forbes*. https://www.forbes.com/sites/tracybrower/2022/07/04/follow-your-passion-really-is-good-advice-3-ways-to-fuel-your-career/
This article provides the reader with further insight into how passion can lead to a happy career.

Roberts, L. M., Spreitzer, G. M., Dutton, J. E., Quinn, R. E., Heaphy, E. D., & Barker, B. (2005, January). *How to play to your strengths*. Harvard Business Review. https://hbr.org/2005/01/how-to-play-to-your-strengths
This article, on the Reflected Best Self method, provides the reader with a better understanding of how strengths can be used to increase career potential.

References

Brower, T., PhD. (2022, July 4). Follow your passion really is good advice: 3 ways to fuel your career. *Forbes.* https://www.forbes.com/sites/tracybrower/2022/07/04/follow-your-passion-really-is-good-advice-3-ways-to-fuel-your-career/

Dobrow Riza, S., & Heller, D. (2015). Follow your heart or your head? A longitudinal study of the facilitating role of calling and ability in the pursuit of a challenging career. *Journal of Applied Psychology, 100*(3), 695–712. https://doi.org/10.1037/a0038011

Elliott, K. (2023, September 26). How to choose a career: Five steps to take when you're stuck. *Forbes.* https://www.forbes.com/sites/forbescoachescouncil/2023/09/26/how-to-choose-a-career-five-steps-to-take-when-youre-stuck/

Flade, P., Asplund, J., & Elliot, G. (2015, October 8). *Employees who use their strengths outperform those who don't.* Gallup.com. https://www.gallup.com/workplace/236561/employees-strengths-outperform-don.aspx

Statista. (2023). Global sports market revenue 2027. *Statista.* https://www-statista.com.oxfordbrookes.idm.oclc.org/statistics/269799/worldwide-revenue-from-sports-merchandising-by-region/

Weight, E. A., Taylor, E., Huml, M. R., & Dixon, M. A. (2021). Working in the sport industry: A classification of human capital archetypes. *Journal of Sport Management, 35*(4), 364–378. https://doi.org/10.1123/jsm.2020-0070

Wong, G. (2008). *The comprehensive guide to careers in sports.* Jones & Bartlett Learning.

4
UNDERSTANDING YOUR PATH

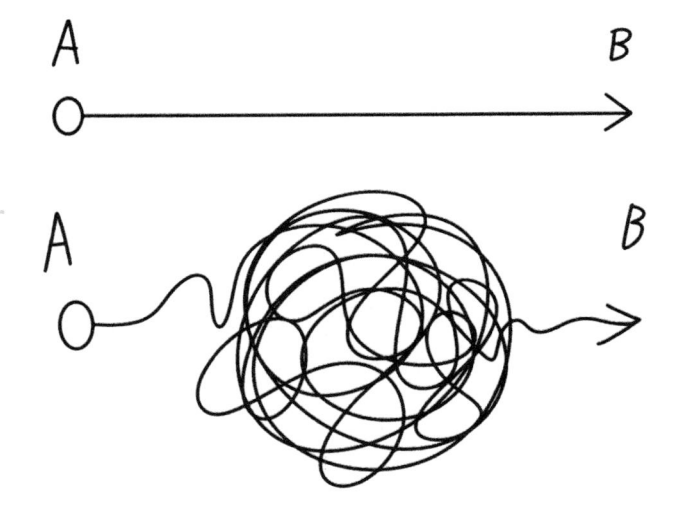

Introduction

From an early age, it is ingrained in many to follow a specific linear path to success. Do well in school; go to university; start a career. This direct type of a path starts at point A and ends at point B. For some, it may be this simple, but for many the path to starting a career is not so direct. This was evident after speaking with a number of sport industry professionals. All of their paths were slightly different, less linear and much more indirect. There was no exact formula for obtaining a position in the sport industry,

DOI: 10.4324/9781003389330-4

only consistent elements of planning and preparation towards achieving a set career goal. The goal was always to get from point A to point B; however, as they would find out, there were stops along the way.

One's path to working in the sport industry can be highly unique and vary from person to person. The reason for variation is based on a number of internal and external factors, such as general interest, skill set, education level, experience, personal circumstances, and opportunity. Despite existing similarities around career aspiration, the combination of varying internal and external factors results in a dynamic and unique path leading to a career in sport.

The sport industry itself offers a variety of diverse career paths. One can work as a coach, an entrepreneur, in journalism, sales, marketing, among others, which leads to a number of different bespoke paths. The industry is continuously becoming more and more global, thus resulting in career opportunities both domestically and internationally. Further, the sport industry is constantly evolving, due to changes in technology, consumer behavior, and consumption, thus leading to alternative career trajectories. Therefore, it may seem overwhelming on how to start, and you may question whether or not you are on the right path to accomplish your career goals. But the truth is, to start, you need to take simply a first step, and the right path itself will follow.

At the commencement speech for the Massachusetts Institute of Technology's (MIT) 2023 graduating class, Mark Rober, an engineer and inventor, told the group to "pick what you think is the best path and just move forward" (Dizikes, 2023). Rober further advised the recent group of graduating MIT students to learn from failure and to view setbacks as a feature of the journey. All of this while also highlighting the importance of fostering developed relationships. Throughout the duration of the commencement speech, Rober reiterated the process of navigating through life one step at a time, and that each step leads to the next step; thus creating your own unique path. This message resonates strongly with those interviewed for this book.

> I tell them (those who ask about working in sport) everyone's journey is different. Don't follow my footsteps because what I'm doing is not a traditional path; but I don't think anyone has a traditional path.
>
> Alexander Khilnani, Senior Director of Yield Strategy, Revenue Innovation and Analytics, NBC Sports and Olympics

~~Career~~ Entrepreneurial Mindset

The main takeaway from this chapter, which cannot be overstated, is the recognition that everyone's path to working in the sport industry is different and unique. Despite this, one should not assume there is a lack of preparation or thought which goes into embarking on and taking a first step towards this path. As you will read in Chapter 5, a specific mindset is needed to continue and push forward on the path towards working in the sport industry. But what about to start? What specific mindset should one be in when ready to embark on this journey?

Traditionally, this would be identified as a career mindset. This type of a mindset is proactive in nature, focusing on developing skills and long-term planning to effectively climb the employment ladder within a single organization. However, this type of mindset and career trajectory is not common within the younger generation in the workforce today. Perna (2023) states that 74% of millennials and Gen Z workers are looking at career and/or job changes within the next year. Today's working environment is not indicative of longevity within the same organization.

This is where having an entrepreneurial mindset comes into play. An entrepreneurial mindset as defined by Daspit et al. (2021) is:

> A cognitive perspective that enables an individual to create value by recognizing and acting on opportunities, making decisions with limited information, and remaining adaptable and resilient in conditions that are often uncertain and complex.

An entrepreneurial mindset aligns more closely with the unique and differing career paths of those working in the sport industry today. This style of thinking is more independent and innovative. There are elements of taking risk, searching for and identifying opportunities, and, ultimately, creating one's own future. Individuals with an entrepreneurial mindset should be comfortable with autonomy and embracing uncertainty, while constantly looking for innovative ways to achieve their goals.

One's entrepreneurial mindset should involve being proactive. Set goals, be intentional with decision-making, and stay on the lookout for opportunities. This type of mindset should be strategic in nature and come with the understanding that a career path is fluid and at times likely to change.

Step 1: Taking Your First Step

To start preparing for working in the sport industry, take a moment to reflect. Begin to identify areas of the industry which are of interest and appealing to you. Think back on the previous chapters from this book and your answered action items. Are the decisions you are making, or planning to make, in alignment with your answers? Next, do you have an area of the sport industry you are interested in working in or are you unsure of what aspect of the industry is desirable? Depending on your answer to this question, either continue with the next section below or skip ahead to **I am Unsure of What I Want to Do in Sport** below.

I Want to Work In/As... (Fill in the blank here: e.g. A Tennis Coach)

You are well on your way! As you have an indication as to which aspect of the sport industry you want to work in, it is now for you to focus on individuals within that field and begin to trace their career paths. For example, take myself as the author of this book. Originally, I wanted to coach and work with athletes; this was the start of my first career. If you were to look me up on LinkedIn, you would be able to take a look at my experiences and note the following in relation to coaching:

- Spent two years as an undergraduate student at university working with USA Team Handball as a video and statistics assistant (volunteer).
- Spent one year as a graduate student at university working for an organization which created and implemented youth sport training/coaching certifications.
- Spent two years post university coaching varsity high school basketball and tennis.
- Obtained a professional coaching certification through the United States Professional Tennis Association (USPTA).
- Spent two years as a tennis professional for a larger sport club franchise in the United States.
- Studied coaching as a part of doctoral education.
- Transitioned to the business side of professional tennis for three years.

These experiences were progressive and built off of each other. This was a very non-direct path to get into coaching, however, each step led to a new opportunity down that path. The point being, you can take these experiences and see a mixture of volunteer work, paid work, work while a student, and further education; all of which opened doors to a variety of opportunities. As mentioned, this path to coaching was unique for me. If you research others who were/are coaches, you will see a number of different ways in which they got their start and achieved their goals within the profession. Take note of the similarities and comparisons to your experiences, and use that information to further aid in your preparation.

The next step is to build your experience in that chosen aspect of the sport industry. Of the interviewees for this book, those with a strong idea of what they wanted to do in the industry early on continued to focus on what they could do to gain more experience and hone their craft with each opportunity presented to them. Alex Strafer, Account Executive Group Sales at DC

United, introduced in Chapter 3, recognized while at university his potential for a path towards sales:

> (While in university) I got really comfortable with talking to people and especially working with (my professors). I think I kind of grew into knowing my spot...; that I knew my words could take me to somewhere special. So that's what I was trying to find. I interned in the Cape Cod Baseball League, working with the Y-D (Yarmouth-Dennis) Red Sox; which kind of threw me into doing operations as well as...learning how to talk to clients and learning how to find out that I was good at talking to people.
>
> (Following the internship, a) different opportunity with the ECHL (East Coast Hockey League) Worcester Railers (came about), which is an affiliate of the New York Islanders (National Hockey League). Within a year, I was growing really well. My sales started to go really strong. They noticed I could talk to people really well, put me in charge of, you know, season tickets, group sales, sponsorships, marketing, a little bit of everything.
> *Alex Strafer, Account Executive Group Sales,*
DC United

Recognize a skill which you feel as though you are good at? One which can translate well into the sport industry? Use this as your starting point on your journey and career path.

If you have just finished reading this section, you can skip **I am Unsure of What I Want to Do in Sport** and head towards to following section: **Step 2: Preparation and Planning.**

I am Unsure of What I Want to Do in Sport

It is perfectly fine to acknowledge that you are unsure of the specific area of the sport industry you want to work in. As identified previously, the industry itself is vast with numerous avenues to choose from. Finding the answer to understanding where you want to go in the sport industry begins with research and experience. At the very least, you can begin researching careers of interest, or simply identify aspects of the sport industry which you find exciting and desirable. Utilize your network, or ability to network, to learn more about aspects of the industry that are of interest. Reach out to current or former professors (who most likely have worked in the industry) to gauge their experiences. Use social media resources, such as LinkedIn, to connect with industry professionals to obtain current insights into the field. When discussing the idea of cold emailing or messaging industry professionals, it was felt this practice was appreciated and accepted:

...mainly it was reaching out to people in (job) titles at that time that I felt I would be interested in and letting them know that I just want to have a conversation. You know, I just want to have a talk, a chat about what they do and better understand what they do. And many people were very willing to have that, you know, especially with students. People know that they were in that position five, 10, 15 years ago. And they can relate and are more than willing to give back pieces of information or just explain their day-to-day; their week to week; their priorities.

Theren Bullock, Foundation Senior Manager,
Fédération Internationale de Basketball (FIBA)

Further, this practice resulted in higher levels of insight in relation to preparing for a career in sport; helping to determine whether or not a career choice was right for them, while then helping to be placed in the right direction.

And at that time, I was able to understand what I did or did not want to do, not 100%, but there were a few (job) titles that I was like I would love to do that. And after speaking with someone in that role, I was like that's a great job for that person, but I would not be a good fit for that. I would have never known that if I would not have reached out and had those conversations.

(For example) I was talking with someone that was in charge of scouting for an NBA team because I thought that would really be something I would be interested in. But after speaking to that person I just felt it wasn't for me, but he put me in contact with someone that was working more in basketball and social development and it's someone that he put me in contact with that I still consider a mentor to this day, you know, and that it would have never happened if I would not have reached out initially to the first person.

Theren Bullock, Foundation Senior Manager,
Fédération Internationale de Basketball (FIBA)

Step 2: Preparation and Planning

The majority of the interviewees for this book acknowledged the fact that their actual journey to a career in sport was not what they perceived it would be when starting out; they all prepared, however, and took advantage of opportunities when they were presented with them.

There's no master plan. You need to be motivated, especially in the first couple of years. I didn't have a master plan behind it (career path). It is being authentic and really trying hard. Usually, life and time will bring up some good opportunities for you. But you need to be ready to grab these opportunities…and get out of your comfort zone.

Ole Schilke, Executive Director, Sportfive

Despite the potential indirect nature of your career path, it is still essential to prepare and plan. You may ultimately deviate from your identified plan, but you will be prepared for the next move when it presents itself. It may be hard to think about and conceptualize much beyond the immediate future, but as you prepare and plan for a career in the sport industry think about a few years down the road. What do the next three to five years look like? Longer term thinking, with regards to your career plan, can be beneficial. According to McNevin (2023), a longer-term career plan can reduce stress related to your career, increase your overall employability, and connect you more closely with your path and overall purpose.

Further, focusing on your career one year at a time may set yourself with goals which are unrealistic to accomplish in such a short period of time (McNevin, 2023). Relating back to Chapter 2 which highlighted the skills needed to work in the sport industry, soft skills, specifically, are developed continuously over periods of time. You may aim to improve your communication, for example, over the course of a year but this skill will not be fully mastered or accomplished after simply 12 months of effort.

In addition to identifying an area of the sport industry which is of interest, it is also important to prioritize areas of importance within a job opportunity and career. According to the career and development team at the Massachusetts Institute of Technology (MIT) when embarking on a career it is necessary to prioritize your skills, your interests, and what is of importance to you (MIT, 2022). For example, salary, work life balance, or the ability to grow and develop within an organization. It is easy to overlook some of these when an opportunity to step into the sport industry comes about, however, understanding your job priorities can greatly help in your decision-making.

Overthinking Your Path and How Not to Do It

I'm quite satisfied with the route that I've taken and how it has turned out. I would always, you know, jump on any chance, **don't overthink it**…for me, it has been a very cool journey, you know, to just say yes, to the opportunity you're presented with because you never know what will come next. I mean, this sports industry is so connected with so many different industries and it's a huge, huge thing.

Torill Lunde, Business Development Manager, Joymo

Whether you have a strong understanding of your ideal career or you are simply trying to figure it out, it is easy to overthink the process surrounding your impending career path. Throughout your career there will be plenty of times in which you need to make a decision. Early on, the weight of making a decision, and the impact it may have on your career, can be perceived as quite heavy. Will the decision you make be the right one? Will it lead to my ideal career? Will another opportunity present itself?

Wilding (2024) identifies three types of overthinking: Rumination, future tripping, and overanalyzing. Each of these three versions of overthinking can occur along your journey to working in sport. Rumination involves dwelling, constantly, on past events, specifically, negative ones. This could occur early on in your career when applying for jobs and facing the prospect of early career rejection. Future tripping is the opposite of rumination. Instead of focusing on the past, one focuses relentlessly on the future. Throughout your career it is likely you will be focusing on the future and your progression, and thus are subject to overthinking in this regard. Overanalyzing is the result of diving too deep into a thought or situation. Early on in your career you will be applying for jobs, figuring out the best way to get your foot in the door, and researching the paths of others. Therefore, overanalyzing may be likely here. From experience, the process of decision-making is hard, and overthinking a decision only makes it harder.

Beyond adding difficulty and frustration to the decision-making processes, overthinking can actually impact your physical well-being in a negative way. In a study published by the *Journal of Abnormal Psychology*, Michl et al. (2013) link overthinking with higher levels of depression and anxiety. In the book, *Act Before You OverThink: Make Decisions Easier and Liberate Your Mind*, by Lison Mage and Guy Langlois (2022), the authors conclude, after conducting 365 interviews with identified overthinkers, that there are three common misconceptions around overthinking. The first, that overthinking enhances thinking; the second, overthinking bears no consequence on the thinker; and the third, overthinking is an integral part of the decision-making process.

Therefore, as you are preparing for and planning your next steps along your journey keep in mind these three takeaways. Overthinking your decisions will not enhance your overall level of thinking. Overthinking, if done consistently, will be negatively impactful, and that overthinking should not be viewed as a necessary part of your decision-making process.

So, what can be done to prevent the cycle of thinking too much, leading to stress and overwhelm? An easy first step is to focus what you have control over versus what you cannot control. For example, you can control applying for jobs and preparing for interviews, but you cannot control the decision-making of a hiring manager. Additionally, Wilding (2021) outlines five strategies for limiting overthinking and for encouraging more effective decision-making.

Move away from decision-making through perfectionism. Trying to make the perfect decision is overwhelming. Simply approaching decision-making with a right or wrong decision mentality is ineffective and therefore should be replaced with a progressive form of thinking. For example, which decision, based on the information acquired, is the most logical next step in relation to your goals and objectives?

Additionally, when the need to make a decision occurs, give thought to the overall level of impact the decision will have. What is the size of the decision? In terms of goals and objectives, how much of these will be impacted by the decision? Consider decisions in relation to time. Will the decision impact me X number of years into the future?

Embrace your intuition and listen to the initial decision-making response your brain provides in context. If time is short, and there is a limited amount of data available to consider, utilize your intuition as a valuable decision-making tool.

Decision-making is a daily task, from what to eat for breakfast to which route to take to work. As the day goes on, more and more decisions are made, resulting in decision fatigue. When fatigued, you are more likely to overthink your decisions. Therefore, to limit decision fatigue, rely on routines to make easy decisions, while also removing some decisions altogether.

Finally, Wilding (2021) highlights Parkinson's Law where the duration of a task expands to fill the allotted amount of time for completion. If, for example, you are working on a project and have two months to complete it, the project will take two months to complete; even if the amount of work needed to finish the project does not actually require two months of time to finish it. Therefore, be conscious of the amount of time you have given yourself to make a decision, as lengthier deadlines can result in procrastination and tighter deadlines can lead to quicker decision-making.

Importance of Relationships

> There are so many people that help us to get to where we're at. And so, one of the early lessons (I learned) was…just treating people well, being interested in people. It's so valuable because, you know, that's really what makes the world turn, right. It's relationships. And as you can see from the way my pathway ended up being, it's the relationships that got me to where I got.
>
> *Dr Larry Lauer, Director of Mental Performance, United States Tennis Association (USTA)*

When discussing relationships in this section, the focus will be on developing impactful relationships. The importance here is not so much around simply networking and connecting, but more so on identifying individuals with whom relationships can have a significant impact on your career. Fernandez and Velasquez (2021) liken these individuals to your very own board of directors; aimed with helping an early career professional navigate and excel along their journey. This customizable board of directors consists of five key individuals: The mentor, the sponsor, the partner, the competitor, and the mentee. Each of these serve different roles along the career journey, and therefore it is beneficial to identify who these individuals could be and begin to cultivate relationships with them as soon as possible. Fernandez and Velasquez (2021) define each of the individuals as follows:

A mentor serves as a guide along the journey. Someone who can offer invaluable insight and advice from previous experiences. Someone who can provide direction and support while also being honest along the way. To find a mentor, look for individuals who have had a career path you would like to also achieve and showcase to that person your willingness to learn, develop, and grow.

I had great mentors.
Theren Bullock, Foundation Senior Manager,
Fédération Internationale de Basketball (FIBA)

A sponsor, contrary to a mentor, act mainly as advocates for your career advancement. Sponsors are usually influential within an organization and therefore can use that influence to create opportunities. When you get your chance in the sport industry, the best way to attract a sponsor is through demonstrating the ability to do your job well and to showcase potential for growth. It can be beneficial here as well to seek out a potential sponsor and articulate your career aspirations within the organization.

Your mentor and sponsor are most likely going to be in a higher position than yourself, and therefore it is advised to identify a partner; someone with whom you can collaborate with and support. Seek an individual who has similar strengths and goals in order to be able to work together and advocate for each other.

The partner may also fit into the role of the next individual, the competitor. Healthy competition can lead to growth and continued innovation. The competitor here is an ally with whom combined performance can lead to overall success. Identify a competitor who shares similar ideals and goals.

The final personal board of directors' member is the mentee. It is your turn to teach and develop leadership skills. There is an element here of giving back from what you have been given, along with the development of key leadership and communication skills. The role of you becoming a mentor may happen later in your career, however, when the time comes seek a mentee which has a similar likeness to yourself early on: An eagerness to learn, grow, and develop.

Overall, it is essential to develop, cultivate, and manage these key relationships along your sport career journey. A diverse group of professional relationships can provide you with significant support and guidance along the way, while also creating increased opportunities for growth and advancement throughout your career.

Conclusion

Your path to working in the sport industry is exactly as it is written; your path. Each journey, despite some similarities, is different and unique to the person embarking on it. As you make a start on the journey to working in sport, have a clear idea of where you want to go and of what it is you want. Along the journey keep true to your entrepreneurial mindset; take some risk, think independently, and be creative and innovative. Planning and preparation are a must in the beginning, however, both are continuously relied upon throughout the journey. Continue to formulate and cultivate relationships with your personal board of directors. Despite the non-linear nature in which your path will likely take, continue to visualize each step of the way. If you face a setback or change in direction, be prepared for your next move and keep pushing forward. As you progress, limit your overthinking. Decision-making is a large part of getting started on your journey, and it will be continuously relied upon throughout.

Action Item 7: Mapping Your Path to Working in Sport

The act of visualization as a means of achieving goals and influencing outcomes has been historically linked with success. Visualization techniques were used with our athletes at the United States Tennis Association, and the ideals behind the techniques have been around in sport since the 1960s (Clarey, 2014). Simply visualizing an act can impact and change the makeup of our brain (Begley, 2007). Therefore, visualizing your path and journey towards a career in the sport industry can put yourselves in a better position to achieve it. At the very least, you can begin the process of understanding what your path may look like, the obstacles you may face, and the plan for overcoming those obstacles in the way.

Mind mapping your career is a way to visualize your identified path while tracking progress as it occurs. Further, it is a way for you to identify key skills needed, while planning actionable steps to take. This process enhances creativity and promotes organization, in a way which is clear and strategic.

I have started the career map for you below, shown in Figure 4.1. From here, look to build upon the map itself. Below you will see five categories surrounding a career in sport: Sector, Education, Job Role, Skills Needed, and

Understanding Your Path **67**

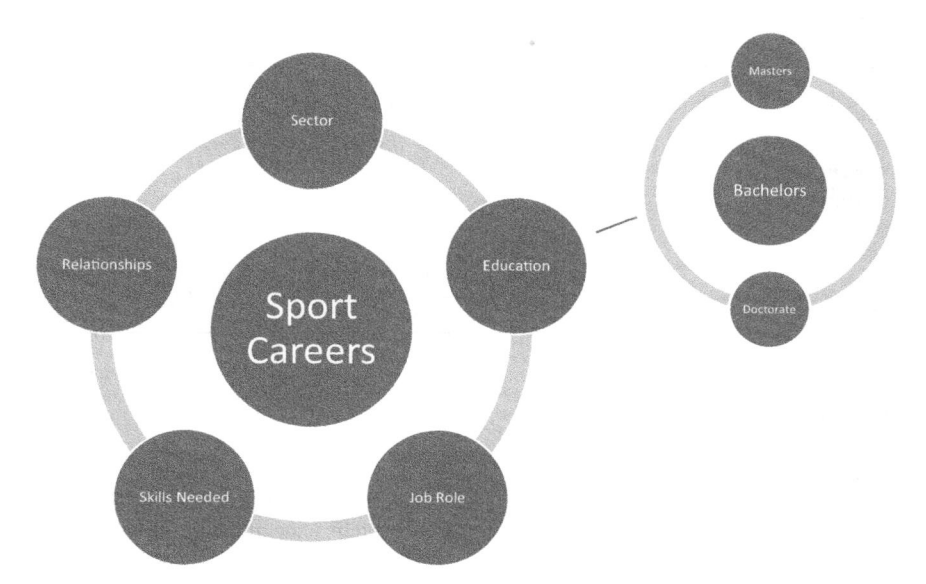

FIGURE 4.1 Sport Careers Mind Map.

Relationships. Your job is to add to and build upon this career map. It may be easier to draw one out on a sheet of paper, or another platform, however, the idea is for you to begin mapping out important aspects of your predicted path. To start, I have built upon education. What is your highest level of education currently? For your ideal position in the industry, do you need a bachelors, masters, or doctorate?

As you progress, focus on the next four sections. Which sector of the sport industry do you want to or could you work in? What are the various job roles you would like or are qualified to have? What skills are needed to obtain those specific job roles? What relationships have you made that you would assign to your personal board of directors, and who else, if anyone, is needed? And finally, what are your next steps, or action items?

Once you have completed your mind map, or have filled it out as best you can for now, begin the visualization process in Table 4.1. Simply close your eyes and visualize your next steps or planned action items and write them down. It is encouraged for you to come back to this mind map and list of action items and update when necessary. As you move forward in your career different opportunities will present themselves. Thus, continue mapping out your current attributes and goals in relation to the presented opportunity and visualize those intended outcomes through identifying actionable next steps.

TABLE 4.1 Visualizing Your Next Steps

Career Map Category	Action Item
*Education	Enroll in and complete a master's degree
*Example	
Sector	
Education	
Job Role	
Skills Needed	
Relationships	

Further Resources

Headspace. (2024). *Visualization meditation.* https://www.headspace.com/meditation/visualization

This article and accompanying meditation exercises will help the reader practice visualization techniques. This can be used to help map out the reader's path to working in sport.

Mage, L., & Langlois, G. (2022). *Act before you overThink: Make decisions easier and liberate your mind.* Lison Mage. https://lisonmage.com/act-before-you-overthink-book/

This book can provide the reader with further insight into limiting career and life overthinking.

McNevin, M. (2023, September 27). *How to develop a 5-Year career plan.* Harvard Business Review. https://hbr.org/2023/09/how-to-develop-a-5-year-career-plan

This article provides the reader with further insight into how to develop a five-year career plan.

References

Begley, S. (2007, January 19). *The brain: How the brain rewires itself.* TIME.com. https://content.time.com/time/magazine/article/0,9171,1580438,00.html

Clarey, C. (2014, February 22). *Olympians use imagery as mental training.* The New York Times. https://www.nytimes.com/2014/02/23/sports/olympics/olympians-use-imagery-as-mental-training.html?_r=0

Daspit, J. J., Fox, C. J., & Findley, S. K. (2021). Entrepreneurial mindset: An integrated definition, a review of current insights, and directions for future research. *Journal of Small Business Management, 61*(1), 12–44. https://doi.org/10.1080/00472778.2021.1907583

Dizikes, P. (2023, June 1). *Mark Rober tells MIT graduates to throw themselves into the unknown.* MIT News | Massachusetts Institute of Technology. https://news.mit.edu/2023/mark-rober-commencement-0601

Fernandez, J., & Velasquez, L. (2021, June 4). *5 relationships you need to build a successful career.* Harvard Business Review. https://hbr.org/2021/06/5-relationships-you-need-to-build-a-successful-career

Mage, L., & Langlois, G. (2022). *Act before you overThink: Make decisions easier and liberate your mind.* Lison Mage.

McNevin, M. (2023, September 27). *How to develop a 5-year career plan.* Harvard Business Review. https://hbr.org/2023/09/how-to-develop-a-5-year-career-plan

Michl, L. C., McLaughlin, K. A., Shepherd, K., & Nolen–Hoeksema, S. (2013). Rumination as a mechanism linking stressful life events to symptoms of depression and anxiety: Longitudinal evidence in early adolescents and adults. *Journal of Abnormal Psychology, 122*(2), 339–352. https://doi.org/10.1037/a0031994

MIT. (2022, November 15). *Make a career plan.* Career Advising & Professional Development | MIT. https://capd.mit.edu/resources/make-a-career-plan/

Perna, M. C. (2023, February 14). Why younger employees will switch jobs for an employer who invests in them. *Forbes.* https://www.forbes.com/sites/markcperna/2023/02/14/why-younger-employees-will-switch-jobs-for-an-employer-who-invests-in-them/?sh=3052994e295c

Wilding, M. (2021, February 10). *How to stop overthinking everything.* Harvard Business Review. https://hbr.org/2021/02/how-to-stop-overthinking-everything

Wilding, M. (2024, February 13). *3 types of overthinking – and how to overcome them.* Harvard Business Review. https://hbr.org/2024/02/3-types-of-overthinking-and-how-to-overcome-them?utm_campaign=hbr&utm_medium=social&utm_source=linkedinnewsletter&tpcc=linkedinnewsletter

5
GROWTH MINDSET AND MOVING FORWARD: ACCEPTING "NO"

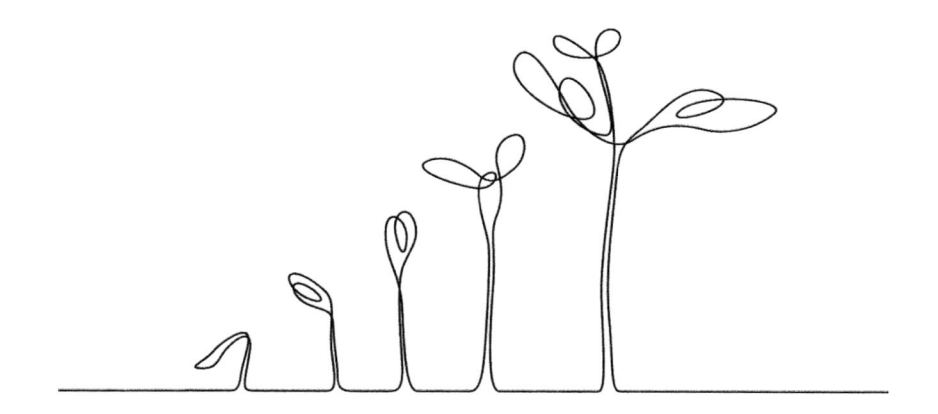

Introduction

Supply and demand are two of the most basic economic principles. Within the labor market, as jobs and industries become more appealing so increases the demand for such jobs. An issue is presented, however, when the supply does not meet the demand. Sport as an industry is growing. Globally, the sport market in 2023 was worth $512 billion, an increase of 5% from 2022 (The Business Research Company, 2023). The size of the industry is expected to grow to just under $624 billion by 2027 (Statista, 2023a). As the industry itself continues to grow, so will the demand and desire to work in sport.

DOI: 10.4324/9781003389330-5

...supply exceeds demand. It's important to recognize that there are far more aspirants than entry-level jobs.

(Sport Business Journal, 2020)

Referring back to Chapter 1, there are hundreds of sport-related degree programs and courses offered at universities globally, resulting in thousands of graduates looking to enter the industry each year. This, of course, does not include those graduating with general marketing, business, or management degrees who also want to work in sport.

To put the number of jobs available into perspective, as of April 2023, there were 6,409 sport-related jobs posted to www.teamworkonline.com (TeamWork Online, 2024), one of the largest and most established online job boards, which currently hosts jobs from the NBA, NFL, and the NHL, among others. This number encompasses part-time, intern, entry-level, manager, director, and senior job roles. In any case, there is a high level of demand for wanting to work in the sport industry, but only so many jobs which are supplied. Of the 6,409 sport-related jobs posted to TeamWork Online, roughly 1,000 were related to entry-level positions. Therefore, it can be expected that many entry-level applicants will not be hired straight away. Instead, most will have to compete with the numerous other applicants applying for the same job; the majority of whom will face their first bits of career adversity.

What's really important in this day and age is (to know) you're going to get turned down more than you get selected. We (USA Football) had a job open recently for 24 hours and had over 300 applications. It's unbelievable. The sports world is incredibly competitive and so you have to be prepared…you're just going to have to keep trying to figure out how and what you need to do to personally grow and develop.

Beth Porreca, Managing Director High Performance and National Teams, USA Football

"No" and Overcoming Adversity

Adversity that I have every day is I have to hear a lot of nos. No, no, no, no…I think that's a bit frustrating, but you know, you just shake the dust off and go to the next one. You need to learn how to deal with no…I mean, I think I always knew that…I think it's a bit of my personality, but with words, especially, you can't take those things personally. So, people can reject you, reject you, reject you, you know…try again or try differently and go a different way. Don't take these things personally…it's not because you're any less good because of that.

Joao Frigerio, Founder, iWorkinSport

In 2020, a group of educators, sport industry executives, and human resource specialists were asked as a part of a panel to give their advice to those looking to have a future in the business of sport. Generally, the answers stemmed around being open-minded, being patient, and presenting yourself in a way which stands out. However, one panelist focused on a negative reality: Rejection. Len Perma, Founder, Chairman, & CEO of Turnkey Sports and Entertainment called for those sport business career seekers to "Be fearless and expect tons of rejection. Persist. Never give up" (*Sport Business Journal*, 2020). The final sentiment from Perma's statement, a cliché synonymous with excellence in sport competition, is just as applicable for when it comes to working in sport. As discussed in Chapter 4, not everyone's path to the sport industry is the same. There are setbacks and rejection. It is how you move forward and progress which determines your fate in the industry.

When 300 people apply for one position with USA Football, the reality is 299 will be told "no." Most likely this number will be much higher as 300 applications were received in the first 24 hours; however, the point remains the same. Many will not even receive a response from the organization applied to, and statistically, you will have a greater chance of the job being offered to a competing candidate than yourself. For many, this may be the first bit of career-specific adversity experienced. How you handle adversity, specifically as an entry-level job applicant, in the sport industry will determine your level of perseverance and drive to succeed.

> I think how you handle adversity is a personal thing. I think for me, as I mentioned that I played sports growing up and so the very first experience I have, was getting cut from the team, or not making a travel team that my friends made, etc.… And so, I think you have to have a mentality. It's okay, maybe I didn't get this role, but why didn't I get it? And what do I have to do to improve to get it next time? So, for me, I'm just constantly looking at opportunities to grow and develop.
>
> *Beth Porreca, Managing Director High Performance and National Teams, USA Football*

Identifying a positive outcome from a moment of adversity is representative of a growth mindset. According to Gleeson (2020), those with a growth mindset welcome challenges, carry on past initial setbacks, view the path to mastery accomplishable through effort, and use feedback as a tool for learning. Dweck (2016) highlights that those with a growth mindset believe they themselves can be developed through working hard, effective strategic planning, and from the input of others. In this context, adversity and specifically being told "no" should be viewed as a moment of growth.

It goes without saying that being told "no" for a first job opportunity in the sport industry will not feel like a positive accomplishment and will often come with an element of sadness, anger, perhaps, and discouragement. Soon after graduating from university, I went through three rounds of interviews with one not-to-be-named NBA team for an entry-level sales position. Soon after the final interview, I was simply informed by a very short email which stated the organization was declining further consideration of my candidacy for the job. Despite the progress and the accomplishment of making it through three rounds of a competitive entry-level sales job, it did not feel like an opportunity for growth. However, it is here in which one needs to carry on past the setback and view the "failure" to secure the job as an opportunity to reflect and focus on what the next steps are. What was learned during those interviews, and how can that knowledge be used to prepare for the next opportunity? After some reflection, I realized that, maybe for me, sales was not going to be my way into the sport industry. It was something I had very little passion for, and furthermore, I had little to no sales experience. However, I did have some coaching experience, and I knew that I enjoyed and wanted to work with athletes. Thus, a moment of career adversity led to a moment of career clarity.

When discussing adversity with those interviewed for this book, there was always a two-part response. The first part acknowledged the difficulty associated with being told "no," and the second part focused on moving forward with a "what's next?" approach.

> I think I applied for 60 jobs and I didn't hear back from at least 50% to 60% of those…For me personally I was trying to make myself stand out even more, whether that be what my volunteering aspects were, or what I wanted to do in the future. I was still thinking the different ways that I would be able to stand out.
>
> *Jonathan Lock, Marketing Executive, Aston Villa Football Club*

> I remember we finished classes in June and I didn't find an internship until November. So, I had a five-month span of time, just struggling to find the right internship, and it was tough. You just need to be resilient. You just need to think, why are you here? Why are you doing this? And just think that and trust yourself that everything, everything is going to be okay. And at the end, all the pieces will be put together.
>
> *Didier Montes Kienle, Manager, Sport Communications and Media Relations, Fédération Équestre Internationale (FEI)*

The path to success in this industry requires effort; on to the next application. Learn from the experience and reflect on any comments or feedback provided during or after the interview(s) which could lead to improving your chances during the next opportunity. If you have a chance to speak with the person who is informing you that the organization is selecting another candidate, do not be afraid to ask for feedback. What should I work on or develop further? Growth is a process and there are always moments for growth.

Action Item 8: Growth Mindset

Below in Table 5.1, is your moment for reflection and growth. You may not have experienced an element of career adversity yet, and that is okay. Simply, save this table for later and fill it in when the time comes. If you have, however, experienced an element of adversity earlier on in your career, take a moment to reflect on the outcome and identify what you can learn from that moment of adversity. Use my example of the entry-level sales position from earlier in the chapter. I did not get the job I applied for, but through that I came to the realization that perhaps sales was just not going to be my path forward and therefore I should focus on the area of the sport industry I truly want to work in.

TABLE 5.1 Growth Mindset

Moment of Adversity	*What Did I Learn?*
–	–
–	–
–	–
–	–
–	–

Opportunity

When asked about the challenges they faced, or how they handled adversity, those whom I interviewed for this book replied with a generally positive answer. Often, we expect adversity and the experiences that come with it, to be negative. However, adversity among this group of individuals was viewed positively; as an opportunity. Instead of fixating on the negatives around why one did not get a job, or was unsuccessful in a particular area, the focus shifted to an opportunity for improvement and growth. This attitude and general sentiment are evident of a growth mindset.

Along with the shift in mindset, it was further noted that you should be ready for when the next opportunity presents itself. The preparation should not stop simply because one door has closed. Be ready for the next door to open and when that opportunity presents itself: Deliver. One very specific piece of advice offered by Dr Larry Lauer, Director of Mental Performance at the United States Tennis Association (USTA), from which he learned early on in his career, was "that when you get a chance you deliver...if you're in front of a team or a camp or something (e.g. Interview panel), you just do a great job with your presentation and be so interactive, engaging, and interesting."

Furthermore, opportunity and preparation need to be viewed hand in hand; together.

> You don't know when you get that opportunity, so make sure you're at that cross section of opportunity and preparation. So, when it does arrive, you're ready.
>
> *Alexander Khilnani, Senior Director of Yield Strategy, Revenue Innovation and Analytics, NBC Sports and Olympics*

So, what can you do to best prepare yourself for an opportunity? Preparation can come in many different forms. A first step post-job rejection would be to simply reflect. Take a minute to reflect on the experience: writing the cover letter, updating the resume, and preparing for and surviving the first interview. What do you feel went well? What could be improved upon? Take this information and use it for the next opportunity.

Seek some feedback. When you are being told you were not successful in obtaining the job, try and remain focused. Follow-up and ask what you can work on. What can you try and improve upon? Based on the feedback provided, is this the moment to improve a skill or to take a class (e.g. LinkedIn Learning) to strengthen your resume or personal profile? This will continue to demonstrate that growth mindset and showcase the effort you are willing to put into making this career a reality.

Keep in mind this element of rejection is not personal. It is not solely indicative of your skills and abilities. It may simply be a case of not being the right fit at that moment in time. Or, there could have been an internal applicant that you were unaware of. The larger meaning here is that there are multiple factors at play. Going back to the case of USA Football, only one out of 300+ applicants would be hired. It is safe to assume the vast majority of those applying were well qualified for the position, but the organization could only choose one.

Stay connected. Reach out to your network. Keep mentors and close contacts updated with your progress. Use these individuals as sounding boards for reflection and preparation. Continue to build upon your network and introduce yourself to new people within the industry. LinkedIn is a great tool for connecting and growing your network. More on growing your network in Chapter 7.

Finally, continue to set goals for yourself and stay determined. Aim to take time to improve your resume, reframe your cover letter, search for new jobs, and then apply. Use your time wisely, and be specific with what you attend to achieve. It could be simply, over the course of a month to break your time down to weekly measures. For example:

Week 1 – Reconnect with my network and search for new job opportunities.
Week 2 – Update my resume and reframe my cover letter (adhere to feedback provided).
Week 3 – Apply for the jobs identified in week 1.
Week 4 – Attend a networking event. Set up and conduct a practice or mock interview.

Each rejection or setback is a moment for opportunity and ultimately puts you one step closer to achieving your dream.

Keeping to Your Path

It is easier to reflect on the process of going from point A to point B in your career when you have actually made it to point B. Experiencing a setback while still at point A is a challenging moment. However, it is important to reiterate that these paths to working in the sport industry are not always linear and do not always go according to plan. Paths, and plans alike, change.

>There's no master plan.
>*Ole Schilke, Executive Director, Sportfive*

>I don't think anyone has a traditional path.
>*Alexander Khilnani, Senior Director of Yield Strategy, Revenue Innovation and Analytics, NBC Sports and Olympics*

Knowing that the path to working in sport is likely to change or will end up being different from the proposed idea is a part of that opportunistic and growth mindset. Keep multiple doors open and present yourself with new ideas for getting started in the industry. You may need to deviate from your initial plan in order for you to achieve it later on in your career.

>Be open, as the position may not be what you went to school for or your end goal, but it's a start.
>*Scott Carmichael, Founder and CEO of Prodigy Search (Sport Business Journal, 2020)*

Your Plan

Chapter 4 identified a two-step method for embarking on a path towards a career in sport. Step one was to take that first step, and step two was to prepare and plan. After experiencing an instance of adversity or a career setback both steps still apply. It is now time to take that second step forward. Through this moment of opportunity, focus on what's next. What can be improved? What can be developed? What can be done differently? As you begin to answer those questions, move on to step two and start to plan and prepare for those next steps.

Preparation and planning are constant themes used when discussing one's sport journey. Identifying a set path requires elements of preparation and planning, and this is no different after experiencing an instance of adversity. In order to keep to your path, and to keep moving forward, you should be prepared for potential career setbacks. According to Goredema (2023), it is imperative to develop a predetermined fallback plan, one that allows you to proceed moving forward with a clear mind. Fallback plans open the door for reflection and provide a fixed and adaptable response to adversity and setbacks. If a moment of adversity is planned for, you can feel ready to efficiently move past the challenge.

Part of this preparation comes in the form of simply identifying obstacles which may present themselves along the way, and how you will address those obstacles as they occur (Goredema, 2023). For example, you have applied for your first position in your sport career. A likely worst-case scenario here would be not hearing back from the organization you applied to. This will then lead to having to start all over: new application, updated cover letter, and waiting. However, if I go into applying for a specific job, knowing there is a possibility I do not hear back from them, what's next?

Action Item 9: Anticipating Challenges

Below is Table 5.2, which can help you to think about challenges you may face along the way, and how to best keep moving forward on your path. To start, think about any challenges you expect to face as you begin your journey. From there, identify the impact this may have on you. Who can you talk with to seek guidance on the situation? Reach out to a mentor or friend who is going through or who has gone through a similar experience. This can help you to identify those next steps for moving forward. Finally, think about the amount of time needed. This may vary depending on the setback or challenge, however, it will keep you organized and prepared.

Reflect on your set path and remember the sentiments from those interviewed for this book. All paths to working in the sport industry are diverse and unique. Yours is not any different. Therefore, reflect on your set path

TABLE 5.2 Anticipating Challenges

Challenge Faced	Impact	Guidance	Next Steps	Time Needed
*Applying for a job and then not hearing back from the organization.	• Self-confidence • Start the process over • Enter another waiting game	• Mentor • Friend • Partner	• Reflect • Updated resume and cover letter • Apply for the next job (or multiple jobs)	• One week

*Example

and keep moving forward. Experiencing setbacks and elements of adversity earlier on in your career is expected. It is not to say that everyone will experience a setback when first getting started, but there is a likelihood of this occurring and therefore it is necessary to accept the possibility of a setback and to be able to continue to push forward.

The Interview

In one sense, the hard part is over. You have gone through the lengthy application process, put forth a strong image of yourself and your skills and abilities, and you have been invited for an interview. Your initial reaction here should be one of confidence and joy. You have made it through one step in the hiring process successfully. Well done! Now it is time to prepare for the actual interview. So, what needs to be done first? As you may have been applying to more than one position at a time, it is imperative to go back and read through the job advertisement again. While re-reading through the job advertisement, carefully consider what skills and experience the sport organization is looking for. Be ready to articulate how you satisfy the needs and wants of the employer. Begin to research more about the sport organization and look into current press releases and/or news surrounding the organization.

> It is amazing to me how unprepared people come to interviews. Basic things, such as mission and vision, but also just read the last five articles the organization has released.
> *Theren Bullock, Foundation Senior Manager,*
> *Fédération Internationale de Basketball (FIBA)*

As you prepare for the interview, it is important to think about how you will be able to stand out. Davis Filippell, President of TeamWork Online, highlights five key recommendations to step up your sport industry interview and stand out during the process. These recommendations focus on **presenting and showcasing** your work and ability. Let the interviewer know if you were referred by a current employee at the organization, or if you can effectively **"name drop"** someone from within. Make the interview a two-way process. **Ask questions** as well as answer them. **Provide insight** and /or recommendations to the organization. Finally, **demonstrate initiative** through pitching ideas (Filippell, 2023).

> …always look at a job interview like a test…understand exactly what they (the organization) are looking for and what the job itself is looking for.
> *Alexander Khilnani, Senior Director of Yield*
> *Strategy, Revenue Innovation and Analytics,*
> *NBC Sports and Olympics*

Throughout the interview you will be asked a variety of questions relating to the organization, the position, and around your skills and qualifications. Be ready to talk about those skills and qualifications and tailor them to align with the position. Present and showcase your skills and potential. For example, if applying for a sales position, emphasize your communication, problem solving, and persuasion skills. Additionally, look to present and showcase your sales work or potential. Bring with you an example of a script you could use when cold calling a potential client. You should be able to confidently talk about the organization in enthusiastic detail. This enthusiasm will translate well in the sport industry.

Be ready to answer the outside of the box type questions as well. The questions which you may not be expecting. Early in his career, Alexander Khilnani, Senior Director of Yield Strategy, Revenue Innovation and Analytics, NBC Sports and Olympics, was interviewed by the New York Mets for a sales position. Alexander was asked a number of questions, the majority of which pertained to the job description, the organization, and his qualities and skill set. However, there was one final question which was unexpected: "How would you say that we're a better family-oriented business than the people across the street (the New York Yankees)?"

Following the question, Alexander stated,

> I sat there probably what felt like a good three hours, just trying to figure out how to answer it. At that point it was probably only 30 seconds, but I didn't have an answer to that question, which was a very important question and I didn't think about it from their perspective (as a historically family-run business). You read through the job description, but you also have to maybe take a step back sometimes.

I mentioned above my previous experience interviewing with an NBA team for a sales position. During one of the three interviews I went on, I was asked, "If you were on a deserted island and you could only have three things with you, what would they be?" During the interview, similarly to Alexander, I had no real idea how to answer this. The question itself is a relatively basic question to answer, but I did not understand the relevance of the question to working in sales, nor its relation to the organization, and therefore I stumbled my way through the answer. It was later on that I realized this type of question, among many others, was a way for the hiring team to learn more about my personality and what is important to me. It was not so much they were seeking insight into my ability to sell, but more so to uncover personality traits and to learn more about who I am as a person (Smith, 2015).

Beyond questions pertaining to the job itself, and some potential outside of the box questions, you will likely be asked specific situational questions relating to the position and your skills and attributes. These types of questions may be framed quite simply: "Can you discuss a time in which you demonstrated leadership qualities?" The question itself is open-ended and allows you to answer in a variety of ways. Discussion could be around leadership from previous experiences as a student, or, from an industry experience. So, how should you prepare for these types of questions? One particular method to use to frame your response is the STAR method (National Careers Service, 2023). STAR stands for **Situation, Task, Action, Result**. Answers using this method should be concise and to the point and should be articulated with a conversational tone, to avoid sounding too robotic or prepared. For example, using the posed question above: "Can you please discuss a time in which you demonstrated leadership qualities?" Using the STAR method, you could answer the question as follows:

Situation: As a volunteer for my local football club, I worked within the marketing department, where the club was experiencing a lack of social media presence. **Task**: I was asked to put forth a plan for implementing social media channels for the club. **Action**: During the first three home matches of the season I surveyed fans as they entered the stadium to obtain specific demographic information, to identify preferred social media channels, and to gauge which type of content would be desired and expected. **Result**: By the midway point of the season the club implemented social media channels on TikTok, X, and Instagram. Fan engagement increased by five percent following the launch of these channels as fans now had the opportunity to interact with the club outside of match days.

During the interview, engage with those in the room, bring energy to the conversation, be inquisitive, and ask questions. Think of the interview more so as a conversation. There should be some back and forth between you and the interviewers. However, as your interview comes to an end there will be the opportunity to ask specific questions to the panel or interviewer. Always have questions prepared to ask as this is your chance to present your further interest in the organization and exhibit your desire to learn more. That being said, your questions should be around the position itself and reflect the research you have done on the organization leading up to the interview. As a sales candidate, you could ask about how advances in technology are impacting customer relationship management, for example. Following their answer, give your thoughts on the question as well. **Provide some insight** around the topic and how the organization could address, in this instance, technological advances on managing customer relationships.

After the interview concludes there is still another step to the process, to follow-up. Typically, you should aim to follow-up with the interviewer within 24–48 hours. A simple email to reiterate your appreciation for the chance to interview and your desire to obtain the position and join the organization goes a long way. Ensure, however, this "thank you" note is authentic and sincere. If, for example, there are four people on the interview panel, each one should receive a unique and personalized thank you; not the same generic message.

Interview Preparation in Today's World

The potential for interview preparation has changed dramatically over the last few years. With the introduction and rise of generative artificial intelligence (AI) models, such as ChatGPT, the ease in which job candidates can practice and prepare for interview questions relating to a specific job role has greatly increased. Various AI tools, such as LinkedIn's AI-powered Interview Prep and Big Interview, can be used to help with practicing the technique of interviewing in general (Harvard University Career Services, 2023), while others also provide opportunities for either AI- or peer-generated feedback.

One easy way, however, to start preparing for interview questions which are specific to the job role in which you are interviewing for is to use ChatGPT (Liscomb, 2023). By simply inserting the job description and prompting the AI software to generate interview questions based on the bullet points included within the job description, ChatGPT will produce a number of interview questions tailored to the job description. To showcase this, I have included a made-up entry-level job posting below for a Sport Marketing Coordinator for XYZ Sports, which I will then insert into ChatGPT and prompt it to generate interview questions.

Job Description

XYZ Sports is looking for its next organized and self-motivating team member to join our brand activation department. The ideal candidate for the role of Sport Marketing Coordinator will have experience creating, developing, managing, and completing sport brand activation campaigns across teams and leagues. This role will work directly with our existing clients in the greater New York City area and contribute to the continued development of our client's sport marketing strategies.

Responsibilities

- Provide support to the management team of assigned clients
- Interact with clients to fully understand their needs and objectives
- Develop brand activation campaigns for each client you are assigned
- Collaborate with the internal teams of each client to develop effective branding materials and content

- Measure the performance of social media marketing campaigns through the utilization of trend analysis across a multitude of social media platforms
- Collaborate with the team at XYZ Sports while bringing forth a positive mindset and leadership mentality

Qualifications

- Bachelor's degree required; master's preferred
- One year or more years of experience in marketing and branding, preferably in the sport industry
- Outstanding communication skills, both oral and written
- You must be hard-working, dedicated, creative, and open
- Knowledge of social media platforms, Microsoft Office, and Canva

Using the made-up Sports Marketing Coordinator position, I copied the job description, responsibilities, and qualifications into ChatGPT and prompted the AI tool to simply generate interview questions for each of the bullet points from within the job description. Further, I prompted ChatGPT to also analyze the job description for ten top keywords. In italics below are the results produced by ChatGPT (OpenAI, 2024):

1. *Provide support to the management team of assigned clients*
   - *Can you describe a time when you provided effective support to a management team in a previous role?*
   - *How do you prioritize tasks when supporting multiple clients simultaneously?*
2. *Interact with clients to fully understand their needs and objectives*
   - *How do you ensure you fully comprehend a client's needs and objectives before initiating a project?*
   - *Can you give an example of a challenging client interaction and how you successfully navigated it?*
3. *Develop brand activation campaigns for each client you are assigned*
   - *What steps do you take when developing a brand activation campaign from concept to execution?*
   - *Can you share an example of a successful brand activation campaign you developed in the past?*
4. *Collaborate with the internal teams of each client to develop effective branding materials and content*
   - *How do you ensure effective collaboration between internal teams and clients during the branding process?*

84 Growth Mindset and Moving Forward

- Can you describe a time when you had to navigate differing opinions or priorities among internal teams and clients? How did you handle it?
5. **Measure the performance of social media marketing campaigns through the utilization of trend analysis across a multitude of social media platforms**
    - What tools and metrics do you use to measure the performance of social media marketing campaigns?
    - Can you provide an example of how you utilized trend analysis to optimize a social media marketing campaign?
6. **Collaborate with the team at XYZ Sports while bringing forth a positive mindset and leadership mentality**
    - How do you foster a positive and collaborative work environment within a team?
    - Can you describe a situation where you demonstrated leadership qualities within a team setting?

Keywords extracted from the job description:

1. *Brand activation*
2. *Sport industry*
3. *Marketing*
4. *Branding*
5. *Communication skills*
6. *Social media platforms*
7. *Microsoft Office*
8. *Canva*
9. *Leadership*
10. *Collaboration*

As you read through the provided questions notice the trends which exist. You are first being asked a knowledge-based question. How do you measure? How do you ensure? What tools and metrics? These questions are then followed by an example or situational-based question. This is where you can refer back to the STAR method for answering.

The ten keywords provided at the end should be thought about when providing answers and engaging in conversation. For example, keyword number six is social media platforms. Your mention of various social media platforms could be included in your answers to question numbers three and five, both of which pertain to developing a campaign (social media could be used here) or measuring performance of specific social media marketing campaigns.

It should be noted that these interview questions should only be used as a means of preparing for your interview. No differently then if you asked a friend to read through the job description and conduct a mock interview with you. You may very well experience different types of interview questions compared to those produced by ChatGPT or any other generative AI tool. Similarly, after reading through the job description you may have an additional or different keyword to include compared to the ones provided. This is all perfectly fine as the results from AI tools should be looked at as a starting point for interview question preparation and not an end result.

Conclusion

In 1994, the Green Bay Packers of the NFL released their fourth-string quarterback, Kurt Warner. Warner dreamed of playing in the NFL and unfortunately it appeared as though his dream would be coming to an end. Following his release from the Packers, Warner took a job stocking shelves in a grocery store for $5.50 an hour. Despite all of this, Warner did not give up on playing football professionally. He continued to believe in himself and to advance his skill set. Through opportunities with the Arena Football League and NFL Europe, Warner received another chance in the NFL with the St. Louis Rams. Here he led the club to its first Super Bowl win in 2000 (Moraitis, 2012).

Being told "no" was a significant moment of adversity for Warner. However, this setback was used as an opportunity to continue to develop, to gain experience, and to progress towards obtaining the goal of having a career in the NFL. Sport is a competitive industry to have a career in. There will be moments of adversity and setbacks. Focus on the positives that come along with such a setback and use it as an opportunity to reflect and re-focus towards moving forward.

Action Item 10: Preparing Your STAR Answer

As you prepare for your interview, it is necessary to think about how you will further convey the skills and abilities which were highlighted on your resume (CV) to the person or panel conducting the interview. As discussed, much of this information will be articulated through how you answer the specific situational type questions asked to you. For this action item, reflect on the example provided from earlier in the chapter, and begin thinking

86 Growth Mindset and Moving Forward

about how you would answer a specific situational question asked during your interview. Use the template provided in Table 5.3 below to write out a specific situational question, followed by your answer structured using the STAR method format. This process can be repeated multiple times to account for a variety of situation-specific questions which may be asked, so practice this beyond the exercise below.

TABLE 5.3 The STAR Method

	Example:	Your Turn:
Situational Question:	*"Can you please discuss a time in which you demonstrated leadership qualities?"	
Situation	*Example As a volunteer for my local football club, I worked within the marketing department, where the club was experiencing a lack of social media presence.	
Task	I was asked to put forth a plan for implementing social media channels for the club.	
Action	During the first 3 home matches of the season I surveyed fans as they entered the stadium to obtain specific demographic information, to identify preferred social media channels, and to gauge which type of content would be desired and expected.	
Result	By the midway point of the season the club implemented social media channels on TikTok, X, and Instagram. Fan engagement increased following the launch of these channels as fans now had the opportunity to interact with the club outside of match days.	

Further Resources

ChatGPT. https://chat.openai.com/
The reader can use this free AI software to practice interview questions (as done above in this chapter).
Dweck, C. (2014, November). *The power of believing that you can improve* [Video]. TED Talks. https://www.ted.com/talks/carol_dweck_the_power_of_believing_that _you_can_improve?language=en
The reader can benefit from this introductory talk on Growth Mindset.

References

Dweck, C. (2016, January 13). *What having a "Growth Mindset" actually means.* Harvard Business Review. https://hbr.org/2016/01/what-having-a-growth -mindset-actually-means
Filippell, B. (2023, May 23). Buffy Filippell on LinkedIn: These are great tips. #5 – I still remember when he had just graduated. https://www.linkedin.com /posts/buffy-filippell-a8054a16_these-are-great-tips-5-i-still-remember-activity -7066751604338655232-BC2v/
Gleeson, B. (2020, September 9). 11 ways to turn adversity into opportunity. *Forbes.* https://www.forbes.com/sites/brentgleeson/2020/09/09/11-ways-to-turn -adversity-into-opportunity/?sh=399a972469c1
Goredema, O. (2023, November 7). *A 6-step plan to prepare for any career setback.* Harvard Business Review. https://hbr.org/2023/11/a-6-step-plan-to-prepare-for -any-career-setback
Harvard University Career Services. (2023, December 19). *AI: Interviews and offers.* Harvard FAS | Mignone Center for Career Success. https://careerservices .fas.harvard.edu/ai-interviews-and-offers/
Liscomb, M. (2023, May 24). How to use AI to prepare for a job interview. *BuzzFeed.* https://www.buzzfeed.com/meganeliscomb/ai-job-interview-hack
Moraitis, M. (2012, May 21). Kurt Warner's grocery-store checker to NFL MVP story a tale of perseverance. *Bleacher Report.* https://bleacherreport.com/ articles/1190204-kurt-warners-grocery-store-checker-to-nfl-mvp-story-a-tale-of -perseverance
National Careers Service. (2023). *The STAR method.* https://nationalcareers.service .gov.uk/careers-advice/interview-advice/the-star-method
OpenAI (2024). *ChatGPT* (March 22 version 3.5) [Large language model]. https:// chat.openai.com
Smith, J. (2015, July 1). *17 interview questions that are designed to trick you.* World Economic Forum. https://www.weforum.org/agenda/2015/07/17-interview -questions-that-are-designed-to-trick-you-2/
Sport Business Journal. (2020, May 25). Leaders offer advice for job seekers: 'Persist. Never give up.' *Sport Business Journal.* https://www.sportsbusinessjournal.com/ Journal/Issues/2020/05/25/In-Depth/Wisdom.aspx
Statista. (2023a, July 13). *Global sports market revenue 2027 | Statista.* https:// www.statista.com/statistics/370560/worldwide-sports-market-revenue/
TeamWork Online. (2024, April). *#1 way to find jobs in sports & entertainment.* https://www.teamworkonline.com/
The Business Research Company. (2023, January). *Sports market size, predicting share, trends, growth rate outlook by 2032.* https://www.thebusinessrese archcompany.com/report/sports-global-market-report#:~:text=The%20global %20sports%20market%20size,least%20in%20the%20short%20term

6
GAINING EXPERIENCE
Importance and Where to Start

DOI: 10.4324/9781003389330-6

Introduction

Differentiation, a key personal reflection which informed the context for Chapter 2. How does one differentiate from another when seeking to work in the sport industry? Identifying the key skills needed to work in the industry, along with a plan for showcasing and articulating those skills, was an integral starting point. However, one's experience can be a major differentiator when it comes to selecting an applicant for a position. Gained experience only adds to your overall development and marketability.

Throughout your educational experiences you would have inevitably been told about the importance of developing certain skills needed to be successful in any industry: Communication, organization, time management, goal setting, etc. However, theoretical application is different from practical application in a real-world working environment. Through gained experience, you will have the opportunity to practically develop these skills and many others in alignment with the sport industry. Obtaining practical experience will expose you to what it is like actually working in sport and therefore allow you to become fully immersed with the intricacies of the industry. Each organization you work for will have its own culture, values, and working dynamic. The more experiences you have, the better you will be able to understand the various nuances that come with professional working environments. Thus, further preparing you to work in a variety of sport settings.

> …it helps you to develop soft skills in terms of how to deal with people, how to treat them, how to behave during meetings, to discover different kinds of approaches on how to do things….
>
> *Didier Montes, Manager, Sport Communications and Media Relations, Fédération Équestre Internationale (FEI)*

In addition to applying and testing your current skill set, obtaining experience presents a more organic opportunity for networking. It is beneficial to, as will be discussed further in Chapter 7, build a network. Early in your career, especially during college or university, the process of networking revolves around connecting via social media (e.g. LinkedIn) or through conferences, job fairs, and other types of engagements. However, outside of your professors, for example, many of these connections cannot truly attest to your skills or abilities. As you gain practical working experience, your ability to develop a truer network only strengthens.

> It was around 2001 when I left my football club and then I decided to join the organizing Olympic Committee for the Athens 2004 Olympic Games.

Through my contacts, through my connections, through my experience from my (previous) football club, I knew people who knew other people who needed people, so that's how it happened; I approached someone I knew.

Dr Michael Anagnostou, University Teacher, Loughborough University

Arguably, one of the most valuable aspects of gaining experience early on in your career is being able to explore the different roles one can take in the industry. How will you know what it is like to work in sales, marketing, or coaching if you have not actually done it before? Gaining experience will give you the opportunity to explore and, in a way, test out various roles to see what you like and are truly passionate about. Work experience, whether through an internship or simply volunteering, can significantly add to your confidence. What a better way to prove to yourself and prospective employers that you can work in sport successfully.

A final point to take away from the importance of gaining experience is the fact that employers want it. Entry-level job advertisements will call for some amount of industry-related experience, and therefore despite serving as a potential differentiator from your peers, industry experience is also a requirement for those entry-level positions.

Why Employers Want Entry-Level Experience

Most entry-level positions within the sport industry will call for candidates with some level of experience, usually one year of relevant industry-related experience. Therefore, despite the acquired and developed skill set you may possess from your years of studying at university, actual working knowledge may be where you lack. According to Momen (2021), two-thirds of hiring managers in the sport industry are looking for candidates with experience. The reason being is this demonstrates the candidate is prepared to work in the industry and has a basic level of understanding of the role in which they have applied for. Most entry-level positions will also provide the successful candidate with elements of training and an orientation to the organization; however, there is an expectation that the candidate will come into the organization with the ability to jump into the role from the beginning. Simply, if you are applying for a role as a ticket sales executive, you need to at least understand the importance of sales, how it impacts the organization, communicating with clients (i.e. conversation etiquette), writing a brief script, etc.: The basics.

Additionally, having some experience in a particular area of the sport industry informs the hiring organization that you enjoy, or at the very least, have an interest in that role. Going back to the ticket sales example, if you have not worked in sales before, worked on commission, or have never spent the majority of the day making cold calls, the hiring organization may be hesitant in accepting your desire to engage in ticket sales. For example, a recent job posting for an Inside Sales Representative by Illitch Sports + Entertainment calls for the successful applicant to "meet or exceed a minimum of 75 outgoing cold calls per day in an effort to generate new business" and to "set a minimum of 10 face-to-face appointments per week in an effort to generate new business" (TeamWork Online, 2024). The hiring organization is not going to want to put someone in a job in which they may inevitably be unhappy and decide to take on a different role later on. Hiring and training of employees is expensive. Blatter et al. (2012) state the average hiring cost for organizations is equivalent to 10–17 weeks of salary, depending on the size of the organization, and so employers are going to do their best to ensure a newly hired member of staff is going to make it past their first year. Otherwise, they will have to go through the whole hiring process again.

What are the best ways to go about obtaining experience? The answer may vary depending on the individual. It is understandable that everyone's circumstances are different, and therefore those looking to work in sport may need to be creative in obtaining relevant experience to showcase to employers, prior to applying for entry-level positions. Therefore, below are three distinct paths to obtaining necessary experience. The first method being through an internship or placement opportunity. The second, as a volunteer, and the third, through non-sport specific working opportunities. No matter the path taken here, each can result in valued experience in which you will be able to showcase to potential employers.

Importance of Internships or Placements

Despite the identified benefits of gaining experience in the sport industry early on in a career, the following questions loom: How do I go about gaining some experience? And, what is my starting point? These are important questions to consider. First, gaining experience in the industry should be strategic. Ideally, the experience you aim to acquire should be around an aspect of the sport industry you are interested in and it should ultimately begin to help shape your overall career goals and align with your career interests. If you have not done so already, begin the process of identifying what your skills are, what you are interested in, and what you want to accomplish in your career. From there, begin the search process.

Searching for an internship can occur through two different routes: A traditional route and a non-traditional route. The traditional route would be searching through job boards and company websites as well as through your university internship coordinator (US universities) or placement team (UK universities). This process will highlight the opportunities presently available and the actual process of applying. Understandably, this route will also be quite competitive, especially if it is with a larger or more well-known sport organization. Typically, internships last around 2–3 months and are inclusive of university credit.

The non-traditional route, on the other hand, is more self-directed and unknown. This process involves reaching out to contacts directly about any opportunities they may be aware of, or if they have any contacts who may be aware of current or upcoming internship opportunities. This route also involves a bit of sales. Cold-calling or emailing organizations to express a desire to intern and to see if there are any openings available. More often than not, opportunities which arise from this method have not been advertised.

> ...one professor in Cortland (SUNY Cortland) who got me in contact with the Secretary General at the federation (International Handball Federation), who then just said, do you want to meet for an interview? Let's meet up in Denmark. So, I flew there for my interview. I could speak about handball with passion and they saw that I had also the international experience you needed to probably be able to communicate with all of the different federations and then that just it went really quick because I think they were really looking for someone. So, I then met with the President...and he basically said when can you start?
>
> *Torill Lunde, Business Development Manager, Joymo*

If an internship opportunity presents itself, it is important to fully understand the role you will play within the internship and the practical experience you will obtain prior to agreeing to take on the role. This can be difficult, as much emphasis is placed on gaining experience and therefore when an opportunity is presented it is easy to say "yes." However, it is necessary to ensure the internship is going to aid in your career development while also progressing you along your path. Hawzen et al. (2018) highlights an unfortunate theme within sport industry-related internships, accepting below standard working conditions for an opportunity to intern with a sport organization. Much of this accepted tradeoff is sold as an opening to gain experience within an industry in which you are truly passionate about. Therefore, despite the attractiveness of an opening in the sport industry, ask questions and ensure this is the best opportunity for you at that time.

Volunteering

Lord Sebastian Coe, the London 2012 Organizing Committee Chairman once referred to volunteers as "the lifeblood of the Olympic Games" (IOC,

2024). Volunteers play a key role in the operation of the sport industry, especially when it comes to mega events. For the upcoming 2024 summer Olympic Games in Paris, it is expected that 45,000 volunteers will be recruited to help with the operations of the Games and its overall success (Paris 2024, 2024). Volunteering may help the sport industry operate, but the volunteers themselves can also obtain a valuable return. Volunteering can provide you with demonstratable experience to add to your resume, newly developed skills, and an opportunity to network with others.

> Sometimes opportunities come in the least expected way. So, for that I would advise if you want, if you can go and volunteer for sports events, it can get you in touch with people that are already working in the industry and you never know what's going to happen.
> *Didier Montes Kienle, Manager, Sport Communications and Media Relations, Fédération Équestre Internationale (FEI)*

According to the London School of Economics (2024), a study conducted with 200 businesses highlighted that 73% of employers would hire candidates with volunteering experience, 94% of employers think volunteering develops skills, and 94% of employees who volunteered benefited from obtaining a first job, increasing their salary, or gaining a promotion.

Physically working in sport is different from learning, or in this instance reading, about working in sport. The practicalities of working in the industry differ from the theories associated with explaining what it is like to work in sport. The theories themselves are very important towards understanding how to operate within a sport organization or how to better engage with fans, for example. However, you will not fully understand what it is like to work in sport until you have actually done so. Thus, what better way to experience working in the industry then through a volunteering opportunity.

When asked about the role volunteering played in preparation for entering the actual job market upon graduation from university, Jonathan Lock a Marketing Executive at Aston Villa Football Club stated, "It helped me to see how fast the environment was. I was learning about the behind the scenes aspects. You see a football club from a fan perspective or from the outside, you don't realize how much is going on behind the scenes…how fast-paced you need to be and how much you need to learn." Volunteering could also lead to future opportunities within the organization. Taking on a volunteering role shows your commitment to wanting to work in the industry, and it can be used as an audition for those in hiring positions.

> My manager has been here 15 years. He's worked his way up from fans squad which is just volunteering on a match day and worked his way up through the department of a job roles.
>
> *Jonathan Lock, Marketing Executive,*
> *Aston Villa Football Club*

There are a few ways to go about identifying and securing a volunteering opportunity. To start, look local. Can you simply volunteer at a local sporting event? It could be at a youth department, community recreation center, or for the city 5k. Chances are there is an opportunity to get involved in some capacity at the local level. Next, if you are a university student, speak with the athletics or sport department to gauge interest in taking on a volunteer as there are many jobs to be done in running university athletics events. When reflecting on volunteering as a sport management undergraduate student, Alexander Khilnani, Senior Director of Yield Strategy, Revenue Innovation and Analytics, NBC Sports and Olympics, highlighted the variety of roles he took on, while emphasizing the benefits of the various experiences.

> …you could do anything from we sold hot dogs together at the concession stand at sporting events to at hockey games every time our team scored a goal, I would blow the horn that went off to working the field and events for our college athletic teams. I think just understanding what it takes to work in some of these organizations, because it also teaches you about the collaboration a little bit more and the partnership that you need to make things work well. Just understanding the nitty gritty and I think it was also a great experience in confirming what aspects that I wanted to get involved with, right. There are people that we went to college with that loved running facilities and events and for me that wasn't what I wanted to do. I tried it out and I'm happy I tried it out but it wasn't for me.

If you are looking for a grander experience, many larger mega-style events, such as the Olympics, will seek numerous volunteers. These positions will be advertised more specifically, on an official website or job board. There you will find descriptions of the various roles and positions available, with an explanation of the application process. You may not have the opportunity to try out a variety of roles within the volunteering experience, as these positions are advertised and hired just like a traditional job role.

As you delve into outlining a path towards working in the sport industry, take advantage of volunteer opportunities. These positions will provide valuable working experience, enhance your resume, and develop your industry network. Volunteering, no matter how big or small an opportunity, is a way to get started and get a foot in the door of the sport industry.

Non-Sport Experience

The preparation and constant push to land a job in the sport industry has been a theme of this book, and despite best efforts, there is a realistic chance that landing a job in the industry does not immediately happen early on in your career. At first instance, this may seem discouraging and you may feel as though you should ignore opportunities outside of sport and wait for a break in the industry to present itself. However, work outside of the sport industry can provide an opportunity to gain meaningful experience which is still relevant to your overall career goals.

> If you cannot land a job in sports, find a job in another industry with the same qualifications. For example, if you wanted to work on the marketing side of sports, find a marketing agency, ad agency or a marketing department of another company. This will also help you keep up in the sector.
> *Alexander Khilnani, Senior Director of Yield*
> *Strategy, Revenue Innovation and Analytics,*
> *NBC Sports and Olympics*

This is where having an idea of the type of work you want to do in the sport industry is useful. If you are unable to get your foot in the door right away with a sport organization, focus on building experience within the area of the sport industry you aim to work in. Use the non-sport specific experience to build upon a skill set which will then transfer back to the sport industry. Keep in mind, if and when you are hired for a non-sport specific job role, the hiring manager is hiring you to work for them, and not to simply develop your skill set.

The following is an anecdotal story of failure within non-sport specific sales, but a story, none-the-less, with an important lesson. Early on in my career, I envisioned sales as the way to get started. One of the very first jobs I applied for following university was with Madison Square Garden (yes, a sport organization). The job was to sell tickets for non-sport-related events. This involved selling tickets for the Radio City Rockettes and their annual Christmas Spectacular. It was not what I truly wanted to do, but I figured at the very least I would get my foot in the door and then be able to move on from that role into a sport-specific opportunity. However, this thought process came across quite evidently during the actual interview, and the hiring manager could sense I was using the job as a stepping stone to move on, and not as an opportunity to work hard and develop a sales specific skill set. Unfortunately, I was not selected for the role, and at first, I could not see why. Upon greater reflection, it was apparent that I should have viewed the position as an opportunity to not only gain valuable experience, but to contribute to Madison Square Garden while improving my sales skills. When the time would present itself, I would then be able to use the experience gained and skills developed to transition to a next job, in sport.

Simply, work experience, albeit outside of sport, is better than no experience at all. The majority of principles and concepts, of say marketing, are the same in and out of the sport industry. Those skills are transferrable and therefore what is learned outside of the sport industry can be applied to working inside the sport industry. I have had numerous co-workers during my career in sport who transitioned from outside of the industry. They all could do the job they were hired to do; sport was just the context in which they worked.

What Was Learned?

> …always try to learn…show the interests that you have and explore different things…because a lot of things (skills) are related to a specific event or a specific project.
>
> *Valentin Capelli, Manager Sport Movement Relations, World Anti-Doping Agency (WADA)*

Once you have your foot in the door and you are working in the sport industry in some capacity: Entry-level role, internship, or volunteering opportunity, your work and preparation does not stop. It may be easier to think of internships or placements, and volunteering experiences as roles in which you need to focus on learning and developing, but entry-level roles and beyond should also fall into the same category. Working in sport, at all levels, has a focal point of continuously gaining new knowledge and further developing yourself. It will also become evident that self-development and progression need to be met by understanding the development and progression of the industry too. You will need to continue to develop within and educate yourself around the industry itself. This involves taking the extra initiative and applying it outside of normal working hours.

> Find ways to keep up in the industry. For me, it is not a nine to five job. I currently work 60ish hours per week. In addition, I read Sports Business Journal and the Wall Street Journal to understand how the industry and economy can and will impact what I do.
>
> When I was working as a contractor with the NBA, and my hours were limited by law, I would listen to podcasts and read during my off hours so that I could make more of an impact during the time I was in the office.
>
> *Alexander Khilnani, Senior Director of Yield Strategy, Revenue Innovation and Analytics, NBC Sports and Olympics*

As highlighted in Chapter 2, learning does not stop once you are out of formalized education. Employees within the sport industry need to be lifelong learners and have the mindset of embracing new knowledge. Needed and necessary skills for a particular position within the sport industry have and will continue to change. As Shimkus (2017) identified, the half-life of skills is becoming smaller, and more than one third of skills needed will change in the future. As years pass, certain skills become irrelevant and obsolete, furthering the need for adaptable learners (Zao-Sanders & Schveninger, 2020).

Building the Momentum

As you set off on your path to working in the sport industry, each bit of experience, each opportunity (internship, placement, volunteer, non-sport specific) is a small accomplished milestone. These achievable milestones continue to present themselves throughout your career in ways in which you can continue to build off of them, gaining momentum in the process. Your career momentum is fueled by small wins or moments of success recognizing the hard work you have put in to reach this point. The energy that arrives with moments of success can fuel your next push on your journey and aid in moving past any presented obstacles along the way.

Leonard Armato is the CEO of Management Plus Enterprises, and he has worked on developing brands for such athletes as Shaquille O'Neal and Oscar De La Hoya. Armato (2024) provides a series of steps for maintaining momentum and building a career in sport. Much of what Armato highlights has been discussed throughout this book: Relationships, adversity, and change. Build relationships with those who can and will support you, as relationships can be a key catalyst within your sport career. Embrace failure and push through instances of adversity by having an unrelenting determination to achieve the goals you have set out to. Understand that change, especially in the sport industry, is evident. Therefore, accept the change that presents itself to you and learn from it.

Armato, however, focuses on two other distinct areas important for a career in sport, and for generating momentum: Value and the extraordinary. As you learn and grow with each experience and opportunity along your journey, think about what makes you valuable. This relates back to identifying key differentiators from your peers, and as you continue along the journey, those differentiators become the building blocks of your value proposition. The final point is to work on and with the extraordinary. Ensure that the work you are doing and the people you work and surround yourself with are extraordinary. The idea here is to keep yourself surrounded with individuals who will continuously inspire you along the way through their ideologies, work ethic, and career path. Think back to Chapter 4 and your personal board of directors; those individuals should be extraordinary in their own right.

Conclusion

As you set forth on your journey to working in sport, one of the biggest challenges you will face is getting your foot in the door of a sport organization to obtain vital industry experience. Many entry-level positions will ask for at least one year of relevant working experience, and therefore volunteering and internship or placement opportunities can be vital. Industry-related (both sport and non-sport) experience can ultimately be a key differentiator separating you from your peers while also serving as a needed component to simply apply. Everyone's situation is different and it may be unrealistic to dedicate time towards an internship or volunteering opportunity, for example, if you are currently working in another job. If this is the case, take advantage of the skills that can be learned and developed through non-sport-related experiences. As you gain valuable knowledge and insight along your journey keep reflecting on what you have and are learning. Build your skill set and confidence with each working experience you are a part of and use that momentum to keep pushing forward on your journey.

Action Item 11: Your Plan for Gaining Experience

Table 6.1 is a starting point for you to plan out your path towards gaining experience in the sport industry. The first step is for you to identify the career in sport that you want to have. At this stage, you may have multiple options on your mind, and that is perfectly fine. You can simply choose one, or write one here in the book and then replicate the table on a separate piece of paper to focus on other avenues. You will see below in *italics* the sample I have provided: Tennis Coach. The next step is to locate four specific opportunities which align with your desired career choice: A volunteer opportunity, an internship or placement opportunity, a non-sport specific opportunity, and an entry-level job opportunity. The following columns below correspond to each of the four opportunities listed. You need to identify the experience needed for the opportunity, your current experience level, the application process, your action plan, and why you are interested in the position.

The example below, shown in Table 6.1 in *italics*, is a volunteering position with the Lawn Tennis Association (LTA) (2024) as a Free Park Tennis Activator. The volunteering position requires little to no tennis playing and coaching experience, and the application process involves creating an account on the LTA website and submitting an expression of interest (EOI). I have then compared my (hypothetical) current experience level, followed by my action plan for moving forward with applying for the position. Finally, the last column allows for some insight into why this particular position. What

TABLE 6.1 Your Plan for Gaining Experience

The Career in Sport I Want to Have: Tennis Coach

Type of Job Role	Needed Experience	My Current Experience	Application Process	Action Plan	The Why?
***Volunteer** Free Park Tennis Activator *Example	Little to no playing experience. No coaching experience needed.	Former tennis player. No coaching experiences.	Create an account on the LTA website. Submit a short EOI.	• Create account • Submit EOI • Onboarding • Safeguard training • Resource training	This will give me some needed coaching experience and training. I can develop leadership, communication, and organizational skills.
Volunteer					
Internship					
Non-Sport-Specific Job Role					
Entry-level Job Role					

benefits come from taking on the role? How will this gained experience aid in my sport journey? By taking on this volunteering role, I can obtain needed coaching experience while obtaining beneficial job-related training. Further, through coaching and working with others, I can develop important skills, such as, leadership, communication, and organization.

As mentioned at the beginning of this section, if you are undecided on one particular career path, replicate the below as many times as needed. This will create a useful visual for you. Use the replicated tables to contemplate and reflect on where you are, in terms of your experience and skills, and where you need to be. This will help to identify a career path that you are already naturally leaning towards or will help to showcase the amount of work needed to be done to move in the direction towards where you have a desire to go.

Further Resources

EOSE. (2023). Sport volunteering in Europe: Realities, opportunities and challenges. In *eose.org*. https://www.eose.org/wp-content/uploads/2023/10/V4V_REV11 .pdf?_ga=2.140763890.1309309299.1697150753-1577692769.1684186364&_ gl=1*syh129*_ga*MTU3NzY5Mjc2OS4xNjg0MTg2MzY0*_ga_05DTJ1R5QL *MTY5NzE5MDU5MS4xMS4xLjE2OTcxOTA2ODguNjAuMC4w

A research project led by the European Observatoire of Sport and Employment (EOSE). This report can provide the reader with valuable insight into the role and impact volunteering has on sport in Europe.

Kadavy, D. (2018, July 24). Want the mind of Leonardo Da Vinci? Keep a "to-learn" list. *Medium*. https://medium.com/getting-art-done/want-the-mind-of-leonardo -da-vinci-keep-a-to-learn-list-af9a7cba83e7

This article provides the reader with additional insight into understanding and creating "Learn Lists" similar to that of Leonardo Da Vinci.

Zao-Sanders, M., & Schveninger, C. (2020, March 27). *The simple joy of learning on the job*. Harvard Business Review. https://hbr.org/2020/03/the-simple-joy-of -learning-on-the-job

This article showcases the process of learning as a joyful act.

References

Armato, L. (2024, February 19). 7 keys to building a sports career. *Forbes*. https:// www.forbes.com/sites/leonardarmato/2024/02/06/7-keys-to-building-a-sports -career/?sh=792abaf20a0e

Blatter, M., Muehlemann, S., & Schenker, S. (2012). The costs of hiring skilled workers. *European Economic Review*, 56(1), 20–35. https://doi.org/10.1016/j .euroecorev.2011.08.001

Hatch, R. (2016, September 13). Behind the scenes with the Yankees' traveling secretary. *Thrillist*. https://www.thrillist.com/travel/nation/new-york-yankees -travel-ben-tuliebitz

Hawzen, M. G., McLeod, C. M., Holden, J. T., & Newman, J. I. (2018). Cruel optimism in sport management: Fans, affective labor, and the political economy of internships in the sport industry. *Journal of Sport & Social Issues*, 42(3), 184– 204. https://doi.org/10.1177/0193723518758457

IOC. (2024). *Olympic volunteers.* https://olympics.com/ioc/celebrate-olympic-games/volunteers

Lawn Tennis Association. (2024, March 11). *Running free park tennis.* https://www.lta.org.uk/roles-and-venues/volunteers/free-park-tennis/

London School of Economics. (2024). *Volunteering can be the work experience you need.* LSE. https://info.lse.ac.uk/current-students/careers/information-and-resources/internships-and-work-experience/volunteering-can-be-the-work-experience-you-need

Momen, S. (2021, June 13). *The best ways to build experience within the sports industry.* https://www.iworkinsport.com/insights-detail?id_insight=28

Paris 2024. (2024, January 16). *Paris 2024 – Paris 2024 volunteer programme.* https://www.paris2024.org/en/volunteers/#:~:text=The%20volunteers%20are%20one%20big%20team,-Share&text=In%202024%2C%20there%20will%20be,make%20this%20event%20truly%20unforgettable

Shimkus, D. (2017, August 22). Why your next hire should be an adaptable learner. *HR Dive.* https://www.hrdive.com/news/why-your-next-hire-should-be-an-adaptable-learner/503190/

TeamWork Online. (2024). *Inside sales representative – Ilitch Sports + Entertainment.* https://www.teamworkonline.com/multiple-properties/ilitch-sports/ilitch-sports-ent/inside-sales-representative-2076130

Zao-Sanders, M., & Schveninger, C. (2020, March 27). *The simple joy of learning on the job.* Harvard Business Review. https://hbr.org/2020/03/the-simple-joy-of-learning-on-the-job

7
YOUR "CAREER PLAYBOOK"

Putting It All Together

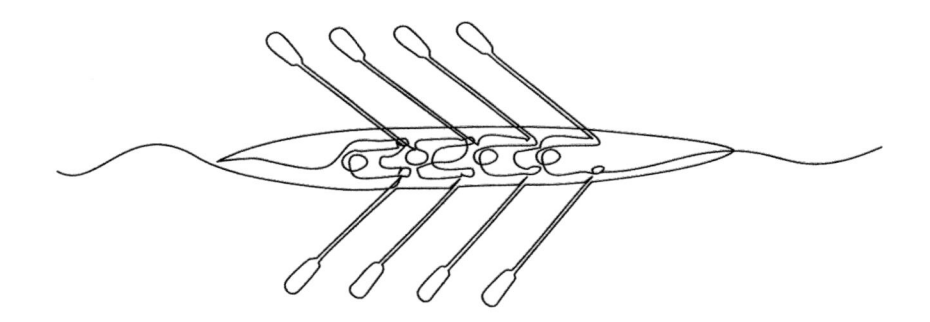

Introduction

You have made it to the final chapter of this book. Along the way a better understanding of sport as an industry and as a career choice was presented. Key themes emerged highlighting what it is actually like to work in the industry from those who are currently or who have spent time working in sport, along with why they wanted to work in the industry in the first place. This was followed by an in-depth approach towards understanding your career path, while accepting there will be some bumps along the way. The final focus was on gaining experience which can support in your journey and career path. So, what is next? This concluding chapter is designed to act as a "career playbook" which aims to help you put it all together. Below there will be sections on practical advice and what the interviewees have learned over their careers, along with multiple action items designed to help formulate a cover letter, CV, and networking.

DOI: 10.4324/9781003389330-7

Networking

> "A network is extremely important in the field of sport; difficult to create, but it's clearly something that is valuable."
>
> *(Valentin Capelli, Manager Sport Movement Relations, World Anti-Doping Agency (WADA)).*

It is fair to say that building a network is important in any career, but this is especially important in the sport industry. Despite the perceived size and scope, the sport industry is quite a small community. One that Valentin Capelli, Manager Sport Movement Relations, World Anti-Doping Agency (WADA), describes as *"extremely difficult to enter."* However, opportunities become more readily available once you have entered the industry. In addition to preparation and the identification of a path, your network is a valuable tool.

So, how does one start to build a network? As Alexander Khilnani, Senior Director of Yield Strategy, Revenue Innovation and Analytics at NBC Sports and Olympics states, "It starts right there in the classroom. Teachers, professors, and your peers are the beginning of your network in the industry." As noted before, your teachers and professors will likely have previous industry experience, or at the very least professional connections, and can therefore provide valuable insight into the sport industry while having the ability to expand your existing network, if appropriate. Further, your peers should not be overlooked. Your classmates or current co-workers will have varying experiences and come from a variety of backgrounds, both of which can enhance or add to the task of networking.

The topic of networking was popular amongst those interviewed for this book. All of the interviewees had their own experiences with the networking process and the way in which their network was built; however, there were some general themes that emerged from our conversations. Those themes formed the basis for how one should go about not only the actual act of networking but also the mindset around the process itself. The following subsections on the rules of networking are derived from those themes.

Simply, there are four rules to keep in mind when it comes to networking:

1. Do not network to network
2. Create and maintain relationships
3. Actively participate
4. Meaningfully connect; do not expect

Do Not Network to Network

The act of networking should not be viewed as transactional. Your approach to networking should not be to simply connect with as many people as possible with the hopes one will be able to give you a job. This is not networking. One easy-to-use social media tool for networking is LinkedIn, and it is very user-friendly to find and connect with people on the platform. However, are you networking or connecting? There is a difference between the two. Take a look at your LinkedIn page and your connections. If you saw any of these connections at an event, would you be able to go up to them and pick up from your last conversation, or would this be the first time you have engaged? Try not to think of the accumulation of your network as a collection of assets to cash in at a later date. At the end of the day, what are your reasons for networking and connecting with others?

Create and Maintain Relationships

When discussing the process of networking early on in a career, Dr Larry Lauer, Director of Mental Performance with the United States Tennis Association (USTA), explained the process of networking as it was presented to him: Build relationships with people by having an interest in them.

> Well, I got to get to know this person so they can give something. They got something that I need. That's not how it was (presented to me). I feel networking is to really get interested in people.

As so much emphasis is placed on networking, sometimes, it's almost taken for granted that a network simply is a set of assets. The process of networking should go beyond the identification of people who could help me get somewhere later in life. There should be more of a human level aligned with the process. Networking is about meeting people, getting to know them, and formulating a relationship with someone within the industry who likely shares many similar interests and values.

Actively Participate

Networking in itself is a process. There are a multitude of ways in which one can go about networking and making that first start. Beyond using LinkedIn or other forms of social media to connect with others, it is imperative to get involved and participate in activities, events, workshops, etc., to engage with people. This is a bit more difficult, but it does not have to be impossible. As Dodds (2023) points out "you're probably already networking." Whether is it simply getting the thoughts of another student or seeking the advice of a friend, it is all a part of networking.

Participation and the ways in which you can actively participate in the process vary. There are the more traditional routes, such as attending in-person events to meet people, and there is the more common approach of taking advantage of today's digital world. A 2024 report from Handshake, in which over 1,200 early career Gen Z'ers were surveyed, showcased high levels of optimism with regard to building a network due to the current digitalization of the world. Further, 67% of this group felt they could make a professional connection without meeting in person (Handshake, 2024). Ultimately it is recommended to adopt a hybrid approach (Dodds, 2023). Initiate building a relationship and connecting with an individual digitally, while also attending face-to-face events with those with similar interests.

Meaningfully Connect; Do Not Expect

Aim to create relationships with people, without the expectation that a connection will provide something to you in return. It is fair to say that you never know where a connection may be years down the road, but the initial thought with connecting with others should not be about what they can or might be able to do for you now or in the future. It is about learning, sharing, and building relationships over time. *New York Times* bestselling author, Tim Sanders, echoes the sentiment of expecting nothing in return when networking. As he states, "This is perhaps one of the hardest things to grasp as a networker. Often, we've been socialized to think that networking is an exchange of value" (Sanders, 2013).

Action Item 12: Building a Network

The steps to building a network can start now. As mentioned earlier, you are most likely networking without realizing you are. Now, it is a matter of building upon and growing your network.

A few years ago, I took a group of post-graduate students to Lausanne, Switzerland, to meet with a number of executives from within the sport industry, as Lausanne is home to numerous international sport federations. While on this trip we had the opportunity to attend an exclusive networking event as a part of THE SPOT, a sport think tank which holds an annual conference in the area. This networking event included many individuals representing organizations such as FIFA, the IOC, and Deloitte, among others. The task presented to the students who attended: How many people can you introduce yourself to and have a conversation with in one hour? This was an uncomfortable and daunting task for many of them, especially in the age of social media connecting. However, it demonstrated the value of what Dr Larry Lauer, Director of Mental Performance with the United States Tennis Association (USTA), mentioned previously: Take an interest and build that relationship. The winning number by the way was 11 conversations over the course of one hour.

> This experience boosted my confidence and helped me map out my future path.
>
> *Anonymous Winning Student*

TABLE 7.1 Let's Network

Name of Contact	Position	Method of Contact	Prepare: Discussion Topic	Reflect: Key Takeaways
*John Doe *Example	Manager, XYZ Sports	LinkedIn	Advice for starting a career in sport.	Network early; Get involved
1				
2				
3				

Your task is similar; to introduce yourself to three people currently working in the sport industry. The method of contact is up to you; however, the challenge is to engage in a conversation with the person and not to just connect via social media platform or email. Below is a table for you to fill out now and then expand upon at a later date. Within Table 7.1, list the name of the three individuals you will contact and their current job title/organization. From there think about the proposed method of contact. It could be LinkedIn, company email, or perhaps you are planning to meet them at a conference or event in person. The final two boxes are for you to identify your discussion topic and any key takeaways from the conversation itself. **Prepare** yourself for what you will discuss. For example, you could focus the conversation around advice for starting out, or how to build a network. **Reflect** on the discussion through identifying specifics highlights or points from the discuss. How can you use this information to better aid in your journey to working in the sport industry or to aid in building a career?

Preparing Your Resume (CV)

It is imperative to take time to prepare the resume, also known as a CV. The resume will be a document which is continuously updated and will help to showcase the applicant prior to an interview. As mentioned previously, the sport industry is highly competitive and therefore it is necessary to have a resume which stands out and highlights sought after hard and soft skills. The following section will provide guidance and insight towards resume preparation, along with tips for structuring a desirable resume.

From experience, resumes tailored for the sport industry should be no more than two pages in length. This may be easier to do early on in your journey; however, as you start to build a career it becomes a bit more challenging to remove, rephrase, or shorten aspects of the resume. In today's post-COVID world, "There are less face-to-face interaction events. It's now more important to look at how you are presenting yourself on job applications and any social media," accordingly to Buffy Filippell, Founder of TeamWork Online (*Sport Business Journal*, 2020). Therefore, in addition to the resume, additional forms of marketable content through social media, such as LinkedIn, Instagram, and job recruitment profiles, among others, are necessary outlets to also present skills and strengths.

When preparing to put together your resume, it is recommended in the first instance, to speak to a professor, lecturer, or advisor. These individuals can help guide you and format your resume according to the most recent sport industry standards. However, it is important to be true to yourself and ensure you are creating a resume that you are happy with, and one which highlights your various skills and talents. You need your resume to be concise and informative but also to stand out from the others.

Below I have put together a sample template of a resume using my experience as an example. There are many links to other templates online, and most likely your college or university sport management department has a sample resume for you to amend with your own information and experiences.

To start, include your name and contact information (email and phone number). In today's ever-expanding world of self-promotion, it would be worth including an element of social media, for example, a LinkedIn profile as well.

Rocco Porreca
Email and Phone Number
LinkedIn and/or Personal Website

Next, include your education. You can see the basic format below. Include the degree, studied subject and graduation year, or expected graduation year, along with the name of the university, location, and any honors awarded.

Education

***Doctor of Education**, Marketing and Management of Sport, January 2016*
United States Sports Academy, Daphne, AL
Dissertation: A Study of the Entry-Level Competencies Considered Most Valuable by Employers in the Big Four (NBA, NFL, NHL, MLB) Sports.
Dissertation Chair: Dr Stephen Butler

***Master of Science**, Sport Management, August 2008*
State University of New York College at Cortland, Cortland, NY

Bachelor of Science, *Sport Management, August 2007*
State University of New York College at Cortland, Cortland, NY
Honors: cum laude

Following education, it is time to list your industry experience. If you do not have any sport-specific industry experience, then look to include any work-related experience here. As you will see from the below, a simple format is used. Included in bold is the job title, followed by company name, location, and length of time. Placed in bullet points below are the various duties and responsibilities associated with the position; ultimately, list what you did at that position. I have underlined various action verbs to start those sentences with. You will notice the action verbs vary and are not all the same to start each bullet point. You may also look to include specific accomplishments here as well, such as: "Assisted in the creation and implementation of USTA Player Development's Advantage Mentoring Program (AMP)." Include any and all relevant work experience. It is understandable that early on in your career, especially if you are just finishing up university, that your sport specific experience may be limited. Be creative here. Include volunteering positions, for example, anything which will help you stand out and demonstrate your ability to be successful in the position you are applying for.

Industry Experience

Assistant – Player Development, *USTA Player Development Incorporated, Boca Raton, FL*
2013–2016

- *Coordinated travel arrangements for the national training program.*
- *Assisted with court scheduling and facility management.*
- *Worked cross-functionally with USTA Coaching Education to aid in the development of coaches and players alike.*
- *Assisted in the creation and implementation of USTA Player Development's Advantage Mentoring Program (AMP).*
- *Organized and administered "life skills" training sessions for USTA junior and professional players on campus.*

Tennis Professional/Tournament Director, *Midtown Athletic Club, Rochester, NY*
2011–2013

- *Responsible for the marketing and promotion of all tennis tournaments held at the club.*
- *Specialized in "10 and Under" junior development training.*

Varsity Tennis and Assistant Varsity Basketball Coach, Hudson City School District, Hudson, NY 2008–2010

- Introduced and marketed the game of tennis to mainly new tennis athletes.
- Focused on tactical training to aid in the development of technical skills.
- Aided in marketing and organizing the tennis program at the Hudson Youth Center.
- Led women's basketball team to back-to-back playoff appearances.
- Prepared multiple basketball athletes to compete at the collegiate level

Director of Summer Sports Camps, Columbia-Greene Community College, Hudson, NY
2008

- Marketed and managed day-to-day operations of youth summer camps by working directly with Columbia-Greene Community College's athletic department, camp counselors, athletes, and parents.

Graduate Assistant, SUNY Youth Sports Institute, Cortland, NY
2007–2008

- Created and marketed youth sport training/coaching certifications across New York State.

Video/Statistics Assistant, USA Team Handball, Cortland, NY
2005–2007

- Video/Statistics Assistant for head coach Christian Latulippe and the USA Team Handball Women's National Team.
- Worked hand-in-hand with USA National Coaches to provide video and statistical analysis of all players.
- Responsible for filming and match breakdown of all home court matches.
- Assisted in creating marketing and promotional materials for all National Team matches at the SUNY Cortland National Training Center.

Following your industry or work-related experience, use the remaining amount of space in your two pages to highlight any honors, awards, or extracurriculars. Perhaps you made the Dean's or President's list, or you were a part of a National Honor Society; any award or recognition which helps showcase your successes while at university is helpful. If you are preparing your resume and you have been out of university for a number of years, then utilize more of this section for continued industry experience, or awards or certifications obtained while working. It is all about being creative in not only highlighting but demonstrating a level of proficiency in the hard and soft skills employers are looking for.

To obtain some insight, when hiring for a position with NBC Sports and the Olympics, Alexander Khilnani states,

> I look for gaps in employment. For young professionals just out of college, I look to see if they were active on campus – clubs, varsity sports. If I don't see a lot of those, especially activities, I look at the employment section. My thought is everyone has different circumstances and if I don't see a lot of activities or club participation, but I see a lot of work (experience), in my head that person (may have) had certain economic restrictions and they worked hard to help pay for school.

As your resume comes together it is necessary to ensure it is tailored towards the position in which you are applying. Your application will need to be submitted online, and in the first instance the application materials will be subjected to a review by an applicant tracking system; a robot which searches for keywords within the resume. Therefore, to pass the first initial scan, specific keywords linked to the position itself need to be included within the resume. Andrew Fennell, the founder and director of StandOut CV, suggests going through the job advertisement and highlighting specific job requirements set out by the organization. Those specific keywords set out in the job description and requirements should be included throughout your resume to ensure the applicant tracking system picks up on them (Fennell, 2022).

Step one is convincing a robot, but step two is convincing a human. After your resume has been scanned by the applicant tracking system and the keywords highlighted on the resume match the job description your resume and application materials will be passed on to a human for review. This next step in the resume review process focuses more so on what the applicant has actually done in their previous work experiences. This is where the hiring manager looks to see how well the applicant has sold him or herself. Experiences which are simply summarized and contain vague expressions will not go far with the human reviewing your resume. Therefore, your experiences, which are usually written as bulleted points below the identified previous employment positions, should naturally contain specific keywords attributed to the applied for job, be specific, and be written in a persuasive manner.

Action Item 13: Applicant Tracking System Keywords

Back in Chapter 2 a sample job advertisement from an NBA team was provided. Within that job advertisement, specific keywords were highlighted, which corresponded to the various hard and soft skills required for the job. Your task now is to go back to that job advertisement and identify specific skills which the employer is asking for and to hypothetically identify the necessary keywords which should be highlighted. From there, you are to write out persuasive and specific bullet points based on your experience. Keep in mind this is just an exercise and you do not need to have actual experience to apply for the example job. This is simply to get you in the mindset of identifying keywords and from there being able to write out effective and specific bullet points to highlight your experience. Please complete the following below in Table 7.2:

- In column one: **Identify** from the job advertisement three required skills
- In column two: **Highlight** the skill or skills you possess which align with the skills asked for in column one
- In column three: **Brainstorm** any and all specific keywords from the required skill identified in column one
- In column four: **Write** an effective resume bullet point which showcases how you possess the skills required while including keywords which the applicant tracking system will pick up on

TABLE 7.2 Skills to Highlight

Identify: Skill Required	*Highlight:* Skill Possessed	*Brainstorm:* Keywords to Include	*Write:* Effective Resume Bullet Point
*Help create content and short posts for sales managers and reps *Example	Social Media Proficiency	Create, content, sales	Created and edited 3–4 Instagram and TikTok posts per week resulting in a 10% increase in social media delivered sales content

Writing the Cover Letter

The cover letter, in addition to your resume, is a complementary document that will be included as a part of your application. The cover letter itself is an additional outlet in which you can look to highlight more of your soft and hard skills, aligning them to the specifications of the position in which you are applying for. It is here that you can really start to separate yourself from the other applicants by being persuasive and selling the fact that you are the best person for the job.

- Linda Spencer, Associate Director of Career Advising and Programming for Harvard University's Extension School, states that on average employers take 7 seconds to review a cover letter (Harvard Extension School, 2012). Because of this, for a cover letter to be effective, it must clearly highlight two key areas (Harvard Extension School, 2012):
- **Why is the applicant the right fit for the job?**
- **What value can the applicant add to the hiring organization?**

As someone will likely skim over the cover letter sent, it is necessary to ensure the answers to the previous key areas are clearly articulated and well presented.

To get started, when writing the cover letter ensure the letter is addressed to a person within the organization. If the hiring manager is not directly listed on the job positing, it would be best to not simply write "To Whom It May Concern." Research the organization and identify a member of staff whom would be most appropriate to address the cover letter to. This could be a representative of the human resources team or a manager from within the department you are interviewing with (e.g. player development).

Your cover letter should start off easy and to the point (McKissen, 2020). Why are you writing the letter, and what is the position you are applying for? Why is the position of interest to you specifically? As an example, I have shared a sample below of my most recent cover letter for an academic job role.

Dear Dr. / Mr. / Ms. Enter Name Here

I would like to put forth a formal expression of interest for the role of Senior Lecturer in Marketing at Business School University. I know that I will bring a motivating and collaborative mindset to the marketing team. Business School University is committed to making a difference through inspiring students and acting as a catalyst for change. The type of atmosphere the University has created, is an ideal working environment for staff and students alike. This is something I truly aim to be a part of.

Keep in mind your cover letter is not a complete summary of your resume. These are two separate documents meant to complement each other. The cover letter should be written in your own voice where you can express your sincere interest in the organization (McKissen, 2019).

> Marketing has always been at the forefront of my teaching. Despite the various roles I have had in higher education working as a business school professor with a sport background, I have always taught marketing in some way, shape, or form. A mentor of mine early in my career told me, "simply, marketing is about creating value; value for brands and organisations alike, no matter the industry." This is something that has always stuck with me, as value creation is at the forefront of business.

Highlighting specific experiences and skills which relate to the position you are applying for can be the next aspect of the cover letter. It is important to ensure specific skills, which align to the position, are clearly presented. The below showcases research accomplishments and potential for future research outputs.

> My current research aligns with The Centre for Business, Society, and Global Challenges at Business School University. As a researcher I am focusing on employability, general marketing theory, sponsorship ethics, and policy implementation, all with a focus in sport. For example, an article I published with the Journal of Business Research focused on marketing and promotional efforts of a questionably unethical act in betting and its impact on consumer engagement. Currently, I am researching the impact cryptocurrency sponsorships on well know events and organisations can have on consumer behaviour.

To conclude, thank the person you have addressed the letter to for their consideration of your application and express your continued enthusiasm for the organization and position one last time.

> I am very excited about this opportunity. I feel as though this position will present opportunities and challenges which will allow me to grow as an academic. The opportunity to conduct research with like-minded individuals, collaborate with an enthusiastic marketing department, and contribute towards the mission and vision of Business School University, is inspiring. I welcome the opportunity to speak with you further about the Senior Lecturer in Marketing position.
> Thank you for your consideration.

Finally, actually sign your name on the cover letter, as opposed to simply writing "Sincerely, Your Name." This can easily be on Microsoft Word or once saved as a PDF document. This will showcase one extra small step to showcasing your professionalism and sincere interest in the position.

Action Item 14: Two Important Questions (and Answers)

As you begin writing your cover letter, reflect back on the two questions presented from Linda Spencer of Harvard University Extension School:

1. Why is the applicant the right fit for the job?
2. What value can the applicant add to the hiring organization?

Your task here is to identify a job you are interested in applying for and to then answer those two questions in Table 7.3 below. As you are writing your answers, keep in mind that your cover letter is going to be skimmed and therefore key phrases and words need to stand out to catch the attention of the reader. Write these keywords and phrases, which should be easily spotted by the reader, in the second column. After you have written those key points, write out the answers to each question with the inclusion of the identified keywords and phrases. These answers should set the foundation for your cover letter and help to put yourself in a stronger position for landing an interview.

***Optional task**: After you have written your cover letter, with the inclusion of keywords and phrases, ask a friend to help out. Share the job advertisement with them to become familiar with the position and then ask for your cover letter to be skimmed. Set a timer for 7 seconds and when time

TABLE 7.3 Two Important Questions

Job Title:		
	Keywords/Phrases to Include	*Answer*
Why are you the right fit for the job?		
What value can you add to the hiring sport organization?		

expires, ask the friend to tell you why they think you are right for the job and what value you can bring. If they can tell you, it means your keywords and phrases were clearly visible and your answers were well articulated. If not, that is okay, just go back and revise your answers!

To Work Is to Learn

The journey to working in the sport industry is that of a unique and individual experience. One of passion, of drive, and of struggles and triumphs. But the journey to working in sport is also that of a journey of learning. Despite the varying experiences along the way, those who have embarked on the path to working in the sport industry have all learned a great deal. Knowledge, which ultimately, could have been beneficial at the beginning of their careers when they were just getting started.

As each interview came to an end, I asked everyone the same final question: "What is something you know now that you wish you knew when you started?" Below are their responses. I hope the answers will provide some clarity and insight as you start your journey, while also saving you the years it took them to obtain this knowledge.

Quotes: What Was Learned

Be more open minded. (And) the value of connections. Understanding how many people in our industry itself are based on connections.

Alexander Khilnani, Senior Director of Yield Strategy, Revenue Innovation and Analytics, NBC Sports and Olympics

To know earlier of what path, I wanted to go down, and (have) allowed myself to maybe take a few different classes that would allow me to have an earlier grasp on selling, taking a few more marketing classes to learn… to know what I wanted to do sooner.

Alex Strafer, Account Executive Group Sales, DC United

I would study a general topic or subject for my bachelor's degree, such as business or marketing, to obtain a well-rounded knowledgebase. Then, I would study something more specific for my master's degree, such as sport business or marketing (paraphrased).

Alvaro Revilla, Client Manager, Goodform

In life and in my career, I think for me the biggest gap between being in a collegiate or a university environment versus being in a real environment is when you're in a real environment, it counts, it's not theoretical anymore. It's not a paper where you talk about a potential marketing plan. It's an actual marketing plan with actual dollars that impacts people's lives, their jobs, their income, their status. You're not in this like theoretical safety zone where you're just trying out ideas to see if they might work. You're in a real life.

Beth Porreca, Managing Director High Performance and National Teams, USA Football

If you want to work in sports…you need to understand how the industry works. That there is a lot of political interest in sport that go beyond the sport itself, that you will only understand them once you are in the industry and sometimes from the outside you see international federations, the IOC, making decisions and you say, why are they doing this? It makes no sense, (but) they are identify all the tensions, all the different interests…There are highly political organizations. Once you understand that, you will understand the impact you can make. Sports is a highly political world with a lot of interests, a lot of sport washing, a lot of different stakeholders…And that if you have the full picture it's going to help you a lot. So,…the sooner you understand that the best your career is going to be.

Didier Montes Kienle, Manager, Sport Communications and Media Relations, Fédération Équestre Internationale (FEI)

I wish I knew how important it was to focus on my technical skills first. I will get hired for my skills and I need to have skills that they need and they are aware that they need.

Dimitrios Politis, Data Analyst, formerly of Nea Salamina Famagusta Football Club, Asteras Tripolis Football Club, and Kallithea Football Club

The best way to keep pushing in your career is to keep learning because you don't always know everything.

Elise Cloutier, Marketing, Youth Program and Business Development Director for Liverpool Football Club International Academies

Connections.

Harsh Khandwala, Sponsorship Executive, Percept Ltd

I learned that perfect is the enemy of good. Don't plan too much and do more.

Joao Frigerio, Founder, iWorkinSport

I think the main bit would be around the work environment. So, unless you've done volunteering opportunities...you don't really understand it until you're here. If I knew what it was like working in office, I think it would have helped me a settle in a lot easier.

Jonathan Lock, Marketing Executive, Aston Villa Football Club

Obviously, life throws a lot of tough situations at you, but just knowing what you truly believe in, I hate to say your heart, but truly believe; go with your gut. Don't question yourself, especially as females, when mostly the people you work with are male. Trust your gut instinct. It'll take you far so.

Karina Klein, Senior Manager Coach and Player Services / Junior Tennis, United States Tennis Association (USTA)

The biggest piece I would change would being a little more assertive and take a little more control of my path and my career. So, it's really just making sure (you're) being assertive and even if you don't know the specific place that you want to end up, just putting myself out there a little more, you know, trying new things a little earlier on.

Kristiana Bennett, formerly of the United States Tennis Association (USTA)

I think go in to situations and take your time and learn from other people and listen to people and understand how they see things, what their goals are and how they work within the system. And that helps you kind of find a role...it's the patience. It's the listening.

Dr Larry Lauer, Director of Mental Performance, United States Tennis Association (USTA)

You can change things. You can change the world. But you cannot change everything. Is not totally under your control; it is very dynamic. So, football where I was working in, you know so many stakeholders so much appeal around the world influences and you cannot resolve the problems of the whole world. But you can contribute.

Dr Michael Anagnostou, University Teacher, Loughborough University

Network and shoot for the stars, not the moon.

Anonymous, Chief Executive Officer

I think that things will fall into place if you believe in it and if you work hard for it. So, it doesn't really matter if you are an early bloomer or late bloomer; it will play out.

Ole Schilke, Executive Director, Sportfive

I still feel like everyone's pathway is different in terms of working in the sports industry. I feel like it's such a unique industry to build a career in. I (also) wish I had some mentors to kind of give me some direction. Like, I feel like everything was based on my judgment and my judgment alone, which. I don't regret at all I definitely feel like mentoring is something that is very important in this industry.

Rissan Norman, Associate Manager – Intelligence Audience, Wasserman

You just learn as you progress, but perhaps I wish I knew that it's not so serious in the sports industry. You perceive everything must be so professional, so very well organized but then you come in and it's not really. You can quickly match the level and progress. This would have given me confidence definitely if I knew this from the beginning.

Timotej Dudas, Event and Project Manager, The International Ski and Snowboard Federation (FIS)

First is the networking, you know, because the networking initiatives that I took started when I was doing my masters and I think it would have been even better if I would have started, I mean, even prior to my undergrad...the networking initiatives that I took started when I was doing my masters and I think it would have been even better if I would have started. I mean, even prior to my undergrad. Perfecting a language, or at least having a base knowledge of another language. I think it's becoming more and more necessary in our world in general, but especially in in sports. So, whatever you can do to differentiate yourself will greatly assist in someone's journey.

Theren Bullock, Foundation Senior Manager, Fédération Internationale de Basketball (FIBA)

I guess it's the thing with, you know, how I've always found myself in those situations where you have to, you know, do that extra work outside of the regular hours. And I think that was, that's something that I might have thought about differently. But then again, you know, when you're young, when you start your career, you don't really think about that much because you don't have that commitment with family and stuff. So that's becoming more and more real to me now.

Torill Lunde, Business Development Manager, Joymo

I realized that there is no single way to get to the position (you aspire to work in).

Valentin Capelli, Manager Sport Movement Relations, World Anti-Doping Agency (WADA)

Action Item 15: Quote(s) of Interest

As you have now read through the first series of quotes on what the interviewees have learned from their journey thus far, highlight one or two quotes which specifically resonate with you. In Table 7.4 identify a specific quote from above and explain why this particular quote stands out to you.

TABLE 7.4 Quote(s) of Interest

Quote	Why Does It Stand Out?

Practical Advice

The aim of this book was to provide those interested in working in the sport industry a type of career guide informed from those who have started from where you are: At the beginning. Hopefully, at this stage you have an idea of what you want to do in the industry, and have a plan for how you are going to get there; with the caveat there may be some bumps along the way. This final part of the book is simply specific pieces of advice given with, you the reader, especially in mind. Below you will find another set of direct quotations from those interviewed for this book. This time, each individual was asked to provide the reader with one final piece of advice. What specific advice can over 20 sport industry professionals give to those looking to enter the sport industry? Quite a lot. I am hopeful that at the very least one of these quotes will resonate with you, the reader, as you begin your journey and embark on a career within the sport industry.

Quotes: One Final Piece of Advice

...preparation...I think it's very underrated and...how seriously to take it.

Alexander Khilnani, Senior Director of Yield Strategy, Revenue Innovation and Analytics, NBC Sports and Olympics

Don't be afraid to take the internship, even if it is unpaid. Just kind of go out there and prove yourself...grab the internship that no one wants to do. It could be life changing.

Alex Strafer, Account Executive Group Sales, DC United

You have to be passionate about it (sport industry). Don't stop learning... keep updated about what different projects are happening in sports, what different clubs are doing...

Alvaro Revilla, Client Manager, Goodform

I think if you want to work in the sport industry that you need to take a long hard look in the mirror and understand, are you ready for high pressure, high volume and quick thinking? And are you the type of person that can make quick decisions on your feet confidently and capably? The people that are most successful in the sports industry are people that have the humility to ask for help, but the confidence to stand behind their decisions when they make them.

Beth Porreca, Managing Director High Performance and National Teams, USA Football

My advice is keep focus on the main goal. The road to achieve your goals is not linear...It's going to be, you know, you go up and you go down, you go up and you go down and then and the struggle, I mean if you get to, I don't say enjoy, but kind of embrace the challenge and the journey to where you want to be. It's going to help you. And of course, you're going to have good days. You're going to have bad days. But sometimes opportunities come in the least expected way. So, for that I would advise if you want if you can go and volunteer for sports events, it can get you in touch with people that are already working in the industry and you never know what's going to happen...expose yourself to opportunities and just embrace a little bit the adversity.

Didier Montes Kienle, Manager, Sport Communications and Media Relations, Fédération Équestre Internationale (FEI)

It's important to develop skills that will further develop your career.

Dimitrios Politis, Data Analyst, formerly of Nea Salamina Famagusta Football Club, Asteras Tripolis Football Club, and Kallithea Football Club

One thing that I was told...is be the best at your position that you have. So, you know, whatever it might be, if you're an intern, be the best intern...so that you can stick out and that people notice you and you kind of move on from there. Some people start out and they're like, oh, I'm just an intern. I'm just going to kind of like cruise by, but if you can stick out and be that best intern, then a lot of opportunities will come from it.

Elise Cloutier, Marketing, Youth Program and Business Development Director, Liverpool Football Club International Academies

You better be good at bringing in sponsors or you better be good at anything which relates to the management of the sports.

Harsh Khandwala, Sponsorship Executive, Percept Ltd

Improve by doing.

Joao Frigerio, Founder, iWorkinSport

It's going to be that you've got to put that effort in. At the start, to reap those rewards further down the line, whether that be in your university or your practices beforehand, you've got to put that effort in...which will help weave into getting noticed or putting more effort into volunteering... making sure that you're doing these opportunities that will help you stand out in the future.

Jonathan Lock, Marketing Executive, Aston Villa Football Club

I would definitely suggest internships to learn. Try different sports, nonprofit versus for profit, because the USTA is nonprofit and there is a big difference in that area. And then also I think what was amazing was with the LA Galaxy, because they were so small...I got to go to different departments and help them. And so, to try to see even within that team or sports company, what you truly want to do, I think because in college is like you get a chance to try all these things like it's a pretty amazing when you truly think about it...but there's not many times in your life that...you can try so many different things.

Karina Klein, Senior Manager Coach and Player Services / Junior Tennis, United States Tennis Association (USTA)

My biggest advice if you're starting out, make the connections and volunteer anywhere you can to see what is out there and also to see what you like to do and what you enjoy and continue to keep your connections and keep that communication going.

Kristiana Bennett, formerly of the United States Tennis Association (USTA)

When you get a shot, do good work, build your knowledge base, develop relationships.

Dr Larry Lauer, Director of Mental Performance, United States Tennis Association (USTA)

You improve, you improve, and that's how it goes. Patience. Resilience. Teamwork.

Dr Michael Anagnostou, University Teacher, Loughborough University

If you want it, go get it.

Anonymous, Chief Executive Officer

You don't need to say yes to everything. Be authentic and stay true to yourself.

Have the mindset of being open. Stay open, whether it's meeting new people, or (simply) listening to people's ideas.

Ole Schilke, Executive Director, Sportfive

Do not look at the money and rather look at what is it in sport that you actually want to do. There's a big difference between what you're passionate about in sport and what you want to do in terms of work in sport.

Rissan Norman, Associate Manager – Intelligence Audience, Wasserman

The sport industry is very broad. So, I think you need to focus on what (area) you want to work in. And in order to find out what you want to work in, it will come from university lecturers and coursework...but particularly from being involved in different areas. So, it's really learning by doing, I would say and exploring.

Timotej Dudas, Event and Project Manager,
The International Ski and Snowboard
Federation (FIS)

I would say it's important to dare. It's important to be over prepared. Everyone wants things easy, especially now more than ever, and sometimes it takes a little bit more time be overprepared and we just expect certain things to happen to us and that's the wrong attitude to have.

Theren Bullock, Foundation Senior Manager,
Fédération Internationale de Basketball (FIBA)

Do whatever you feel passionate about.

Torill Lunde, Business Development Manager,
Joymo

Always try to learn. Stay who you are...everybody is different and you should not try to be as everybody else.

Valentin Capelli, Manager Sport Movement
Relations, World Anti-Doping Agency
(WADA)

Action Item 16: Quote(s) of Interest

As you have now read through the final series of quotes highlighting the interviewees final piece of advice to you the reader, again, highlight one or two quotes which specifically resonate with you. This time, in Table 7.5, highlight the specific quote from above and then explain the key takeaway or message you obtained from the particular quote.

TABLE 7.5 Quote(s) of Interest

Quote	*Key Takeaway or Message?*
–	–
–	–
–	–
–	–
–	–

Conclusion

Ready to begin your sport career? I think you are! The insights and building blocks from each of the seven chapters should leave you feeling prepared to start the journey, with the confidence needed to keep pushing forward. From better understanding the sport industry itself and the various roles which encompass it, to understanding what it is actually like working in sport and the skills needed to be successful, you have the necessary insight to get started.

At the very least, however, I am hopeful you are left with a feeling of inspiration. At the end of each interview, I left the conversation feeling inspired. Each person had their own story to tell, their own successes and failures, their own experiences, and their own path. Yet, despite the differences, there was a genuine sentiment that they would not change a thing. For them, working in the sport industry is and was truly enjoyable. There is no other industry and profession quite like it. I got a sense that regardless of the time and effort it took to get started on their journey, and the lack of assurances that came with embarking on such a career, they were thankful for the opportunity.

Best of luck.

Further Resources

Fennell, A. (2022, September 27). *5 tips to beat the Applicant Tracking System (ATS)*. Forbes. https://www.forbes.com/sites/andrewfennell/2022/09/27/5-tips-to-beat-the-applicant-tracking-system-ats/?sh=4401c8aa2dae

This article provides the reader with further tips on best preparing a resume or CV to pass the applicant tracking systems used by many employers.

iWorkinSport. (2020, May 21). *iWorkinSport LIVE Interview #5: "Building a career in sport," with Daniel Geey* [Video]. YouTube. https://www.youtube.com/watch?v=o9RtqcEJu-M

An interview from iWorkinSport with sport lawyer, Daniel Geey. This interview can inform the reader further on building a career in sport.

Sports Geek Podcast. https://sportsgeekhq.com/sports-geek-podcast/episodes/

A podcast series on the business of sport with insights from the US, UK, and Australia. The reader can benefit from listening to numerous episodes highlighting various individuals in the sport industry and the careers they have had along the way.

References

Dodds, P. (2023, July 27). *Fun ways to network as a newbie*. Harvard Business Review. https://hbr.org/2023/06/fun-ways-to-network-as-a-newbie

Fennell, A. (2022, September 27). *5 tips to beat the Applicant Tracking System (ATS)*. Forbes. https://www.forbes.com/sites/andrewfennell/2022/09/27/5-tips-to-beat-the-applicant-tracking-system-ats/?sh=4401c8aa2dae

Handshake. (2024). The new currency of social capital: How Gen Z builds relationships and finds jobs. In *joinhandshake.com*. https://joinhandshake.com/wp-content/uploads/2021/10/HandshakeNetworkTrends_October2021.pdf

Harvard Extension School. (2012, September 21). *How to write a great resume and cover letter* [Video]. YouTube. https://www.youtube.com/watch?v=PAthQKLhBTs

McKissen, D. (2020, February 27). Here's an example of the perfect cover letter, according to Harvard career experts. *CNBC.* https://www.cnbc.com/2019/07/23/example-of-the-perfect-cover-letter-according-to-harvard-career-experts.html

Sanders, T. (2013, September 20). *Networking mastery tip: Expect nothing in return.* Tim Sanders. https://timsanders.com/networking-mastery-tip-expect-nothing-in-return/

Sport Business Journal. (2020, May 25). Leaders offer advice for job seekers: 'Persist. Nevergive up.' *Sport Business Journal.* https://www.sportsbusinessjournal.com/Journal/Issues/2020/05/25/In-Depth/Wisdom.aspx

APPENDICES

Appendix 1. Table of Interviewees

Name	Industry Title	Sport Organization
Anonymous	Chief Executive Officer	
Alexander Khilnani	Senior Director of Yield Strategy, Revenue Innovation and Analytics	NBC Sports and Olympics
Alex Strafer	Account Executive Group Sales	DC United
Alvaro Revilla	Client Manager	Goodform
Beth Porreca	Managing Director, High Performance and National Teams	USA Football
Didier Montes Kienle	Manager, Sport Communications and Media Relations	Fédération Équestre Internationale (FEI)
Dimitrios Politis	Data Analyst	Formerly of Nea Salamina Famagusta Football Club, Asteras Tripolis Football Club, and Kallithea Football Club

Name	Industry Title	Sport Organization
Elise Cloutier	Marketing, Youth Program and Business Development Director	Liverpool Football Club International Academies
Harsh Khandwala	Sponsorship Executive	Percept Ltd
Joao Frigerio	Founder	iWorkinSport
Jonathan Lock	Marketing Executive	Aston Villa Football Club
Karina Klein	Senior Manager Coach and Player Service/ Junior Tennis	United States Tennis Association (USTA)
Kristiana Bennett	Coordinator, Business Services	Formerly of United States Tennis Association (USTA)
Larry Lauer	Director of Mental Performance	United States Tennis Association (USTA)
Michael Anagnostou	University Teacher	Loughborough University
Ole Schilke	Executive Director	Sportfive
Rissan Norman	Associate Manager – Intelligence Audience	Wasserman
Timotej Dudas	Event and Project Manager	The International Ski and Snowboard Federation (FIS)
Theren Bullock	Foundation Senior Manager	Fédération Internationale de Basketball (FIBA)
Torill Lunde	Business Development Manager	Joymo
Valentin Capelli	Manager Sport Movement Relations	World Anti-Doping Agency (WADA)

Appendix 2. Countries of Which the Interviewees Have Worked In

Asia
India, Singapore, United Arab Emirates

Europe
Belgium, Cyprus, France, Germany, Greece, Italy, Netherlands, Norway, Poland, Slovakia, Spain, Switzerland, United Kingdom

North America
United States of America

South America
Brazil

INDEX

action plan 98, 99
action verbs 108
adaptable 32, 58, 77, 97
adversity 71–74, 77, 79, 85, 97, 121
advice 7, 32, 51, 54–55, 65, 72, 75, 87, 102, 104, 106, 119–120, 122–123
Airbnb 9
analytical thinking, 27
applicant 28, 38, 71–72, 75, 89, 91, 106, 110–112, 114
applicant tracking system, 110–111
application 26, 28, 71–73, 77, 79, 89, 94, 98–99, 107, 110, 112–113
Arena Football League 85
Armato, L. 97
Asia 128
Asteras Tripolis Football Club 116, 121, 127
Aston Villa Football Club 30, 49, 73, 93–94, 117, 121, 127

Belgium 128
blockchain 15
Brazil 128
broadcasting 11
Brooklyn Dodgers 1

Canva 83–84
Cape Cod Baseball League 60
career mindset 58
career path 5–6, 8, 20, 39, 46, 49, 54, 57–63, 65, 97, 100, 102

career playbook 102–124
ChatGPT 82–83, 85
Chicago Blackhawks 8
chief executive 6, 16–17, 22, 48, 118, 122
coaching 3, 6, 13–14, 16, 19, 22, 47, 53, 59, 73, 90, 98–100, 108–109
Coe, S. 92
collaboration 9, 32, 35–36, 83–84, 94
communication 5–6, 8–9, 11–15, 17, 19–22, 31–37, 41, 52, 62, 65, 73, 80, 83–84, 89, 93, 99–100, 116, 121–122, 127
connections 89–90, 103–104, 115, 117, 122
consumer 7–9, 11–12, 15, 22, 35, 51, 57, 113
coursera 41
cover letter 39, 54, 75–78, 102, 112–114
creative thinking 27
creativity 2, 8–9, 15, 31, 36–37, 66
cricket 15
crypto 15, 113
curiosity 27, 30, 52
cv (resume) 28, 39, 85, 102, 106, 110
Cyprus 128

data analytics 6, 9, 20–22
DC United 7, 35, 52, 60, 115, 120, 127
De La Hoya, O. 97
Deloitte 11, 15, 17–18, 24, 105

130 Index

differentiation 27, 89
digitalization 11–12, 15, 17, 105
digital media 11–12
Diversity, equity, and inclusion (DEI) 11, 20
Duolingo 32, 40–41

entrepreneurial mindset 14, 57–58, 66
entrepreneurship 3, 6, 14, 22
entry-level 4, 6, 21, 50, 54, 71–74, 82, 90–91, 96, 98–99, 107
entry-level experience 90
Europe 9, 25, 31, 85, 100, 128
expectations 34, 48–49
extrinsic 51, 54
extrinsic motivator 51, 54

Fédération Équestre Internationale (FEI) 12, 73, 89, 93, 116, 121, 127
Fédération Internationale de Basketball (FIBA) 18, 32–33, 61, 65, 79, 118, 123, 128
Fennell, A. 110, 124
FIBA Foundation 17–19
FIFA 105
FIFA International Masters 38
Formula One 15
France 128

Gen Alpha 12, 15
generative artificial intelligence 82
Gen Z 12, 15, 58, 104, 124
Germany 128
Goodform 9, 21, 115, 120, 127
Greece 128
Green Bay Packers 85
growth mindset 70–87

Handshake 104–105, 124
hard skills 27–28, 36–38, 40, 112
Harvard University 2, 82, 87, 112, 114
Headspace 68
hospitality 7, 41–42

improve 9, 30, 41, 62, 72, 74–77, 87, 121–122
India 128
International Handball Federation 34, 92
International Olympic Committee (IOC) 3, 5, 9, 92, 105, 116
International Ski and Snowboard Federation (FIS) 31, 34, 118, 123, 128

internship 6, 50, 60, 73, 90–92, 96–99, 120–121
interpersonal skills 8, 13–14, 20, 31–32, 35–38, 40, 53
interviewee 8, 29, 44, 59, 61, 102–103, 119, 123, 127–128
intrinsic 51, 54
intrinsic motivator 51, 54
Italy 38, 128
iWorkinSport 15, 71, 101, 117, 121, 124, 127

Joymo 62, 92, 119, 123, 128

Kallithea Football Club 116, 121, 127

LA Galaxy 122
language learning 31, 41
Lewis, M. 20
lifelong learning 27, 29–30
linear 29, 43, 56, 76, 120
LinkedIn 22, 24, 49, 59–60, 69, 75, 82, 87, 89, 103–104, 106–107
Liverpool Football Club 13, 15, 50, 116, 121, 127
London School of Economics 93, 101
long-term goals 10, 45–46
Loughborough University 37, 90, 118, 122, 128

Madison Square Garden 26–27, 95
Major League Baseball 1, 6
Major League Soccer (MLS) 35
Manchester Metropolitan University 38
Mansfield Town Football Club 16
Mason, J. 1–2
Massachusetts Institute of Technology 57, 62, 67
membership 11
mentor 61, 65, 75, 77–78, 108, 113, 118
metaverse 15
Microsoft Office 38, 83–84
Millennial 58
mind mapping 66
mindset 14, 30, 54, 57–58, 66, 68, 70–87, 97, 103, 111–112, 122
misconceptions 48–49, 63
mission 10, 16, 33, 79, 113
momentum 97–98

National Football League (NFL) 21, 25, 34, 71, 85, 87, 107

National Hockey League 8, 60, 71, 107
NBC Sports 29–30, 57, 75–76, 79–80, 94–96, 103, 110, 115, 120, 127
Nea Salamina Famagusta Football Club 116, 121, 127
Netflix 15
Netherlands 128
networking 65, 76, 89, 102–105, 118
New York Knicks 27
New York Rangers 27
New York Yankees 4, 6, 24, 80, 100
NFL Europe 85
Nike 4, 8–9, 25
non-fungible token 15
non-profit sector 4–5, 18
non-sport experience 95
North America 128
Northeastern University 38
Norway 128

O'Malley, W. 1–2
O'Neal, S. 97
Ohio University 2
overthinking 62–63, 66

partnership 11, 18, 21, 25, 47, 94
passion 11, 18, 44–46, 50–55, 73, 92, 115, 120, 122–123
patience 117, 122
Percept Ltd 48, 117, 121, 127
personal board of directors 65–67, 98
personal reflection 89
placement 6, 91, 96–98
planning 57–58, 61, 63, 66, 77, 106
player relations and services 6, 19–20, 22
Plutarch 29
podcast 11, 24, 96, 124
Poland 128
practical experience 89, 92
preparation 2, 33, 57–61, 66, 74–75, 77, 82, 85, 93, 95–96, 103, 106, 120
private sector 3–5
Professional Squash Association 20
public relations 11–12
public sector 3–5

Radford, C. 16
Radio City Rockettes 95
Real Madrid 4
reflection 44, 73–75, 77, 89, 95
rejection 63, 72, 75–76
relationships 7, 35, 52, 57, 64–68, 81, 97, 103–105, 122, 124

resilience 16, 27, 122
Rober, M. 57, 68

salary 5, 41, 50–51, 54, 62, 91, 93
sales 3–8, 15, 21–22, 25–30, 35–39, 42, 47, 52, 57, 59–60, 73–74, 80–81, 90–92, 95, 101, 111, 115, 120, 127
Sanders, T. 105
short-term goals 45–46
Singapore 128
Slovakia 128
social media 12–13, 24, 60, 81, 83–86, 89, 103–107, 111
soft skills 13, 27–28, 31–33, 35–36
South America 128
Spain 31, 128
Spencer, L. 112, 114
Sponsor 9, 16–17, 24, 65, 121
sponsorship 6–10, 22, 35, 37, 47–48, 60, 113, 117, 121
Sport Business Journal 25, 71–72, 76, 87, 107
Sport England 5, 25
Sportfive 34–35, 41–42, 62, 76, 118, 122, 128
sport marketing 8, 25, 34, 82
Sports Geek Podcast 124
THE SPOT 105
St. Louis Rams 85
stakeholder 11–12, 17, 20, 31, 33, 35, 116–117
STAR method 81, 84, 86
strategic plan 10, 72
strategy 2, 5–6, 10–11, 16, 22
SUNY Cortland 92, 109
Super Bowl 7, 85
sustainability 9, 11, 17–18
sustainable development goals 18
Switzerland 32, 38, 105, 128
Syracuse University 37

Tableau 21
Tangible 7, 28, 32
TeamWork Online 41, 71, 79, 107
technological literacy 27
TikTok 12, 15, 81, 86, 111

UK Sport 5, 25
United Arab Emirates 128
United Kingdom 128
United Nations 18, 25
United State Soccer Federation (USSF) 13

United States of America 1, 2, 10, 13–14, 19, 21, 23, 46–47, 51, 53, 59, 64, 66, 75, 104–105, 107, 117, 122, 128
United States Professional Tennis Association (USPTA) 59
United States Sports Academy 107
United States Tennis Association (USTA) 14, 19, 25, 46–47, 53, 64, 75, 104–105, 108, 117, 122, 128
USA Football 10, 25, 34, 50, 71–72, 75, 116, 127
USA Team Handball 59, 109

value 9–10, 17, 25, 32, 34, 36–37, 45–46, 50–51, 58, 89, 91, 97, 104–105, 112–115

value proposition 97
values 10, 17, 36–37, 45, 51, 89, 104
vision 2, 10, 16–17, 33, 79, 113
visualization 21, 66–67
volunteer 6, 13, 73, 81, 86, 90–94, 96–99, 108, 117, 121–122

Wall Street Journal 96
Warner, K. 85, 87
Wasserman 30, 50, 118, 122, 128
Wilson 8
work experience 90, 96, 101, 108, 110
working hours 49, 96
World Anti-Doping Agency (WADA) 44–45, 96, 103, 119, 123, 128

For Product Safety Concerns and Information please contact our EU representative GPSR@taylorandfrancis.com Taylor & Francis Verlag GmbH, Kaufingerstraße 24, 80331 München, Germany

Batch number: 08284892

Printed by Printforce, the Netherlands